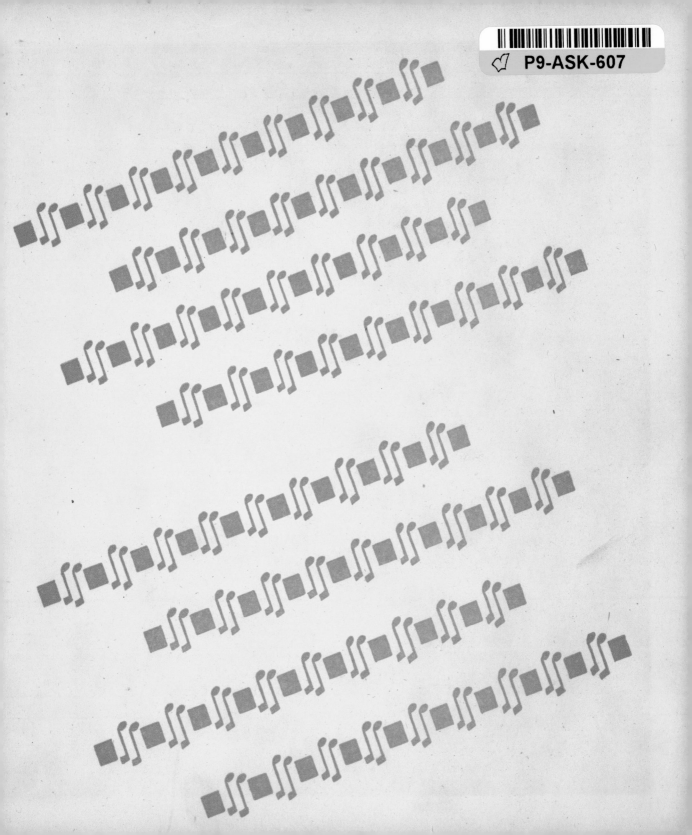

MODERN COMPOSERS
FOR YOUNG PEOPLE

By GLADYS BURCH and JOHN WOLCOTT

FAMOUS COMPOSERS FOR YOUNG PEOPLE

Modern Composers for Young People

GLADYS BURCH

A.S. BARNES & COMPANY ~ NEW YORK

TO
DONALD

CONTENTS

PRONUNCIATION

Bartók (*bar*-tok)

Carpenter (English)

Delius (dee-lius)

Dvorak (*dvor*-zhak*) * (pronounce "zh" like "z" in "azure")

Elgar (*el*-gahr)

Falla (*fah*-ya)

Gershwin (*gersh*-win)

Griffes (*griff*-us)

Humperdinck (*hoom*-per-dink)

Mussorgsky (moo-*sorg*-skee)

Prokofiev (proh-*koff*-yeff)

Ravel (rah-*vel*)

Respighi (res-*pee*-gee*) * ("g" as in "gun")

Rimsky-Korsakov (*rim*-skee *kor*-sa-kof)

Schoenberg (*shoen**-bairg) *(while you keep your mouth rounded as if to pronounce "shoon" try to say "shane" instead)

Scriabin (scree-*ah*-been)

Sibelius (see-*bay*-lee-us)

Strauss (shtrouss)

Stravinsky (strah-*vin*-skee)

Vaughan Williams (English)

MODERN COMPOSERS
FOR YOUNG PEOPLE

MUSSORGSKY

Courtesy of "Musical Courier"

MODEST PETROVITCH MUSSORGSKY

Great Russian Realist

BORN 1839—DIED 1881

AMERICA'S FOLK-SONG WRITER, Stephen Collins Foster, was thirteen years old when on March 21, 1839, at Karevo in the Government of Pskov in far away Russia, another composer of the people—Modest Mussorgsky—was born.

His father, Peter Alexeievitch, was a large landowner, whose own father, an officer of the Imperial Guards, had married a serf. Her name was Irene Yegorova and perhaps it was from this grandmother that Modest Mussorgsky inherited his love for the Russian people. We also know that this fellow-feeling grew through the teaching of his childhood nurse, for in the story of his life, written many years later, he made this statement, "My nurse taught me nearly the whole of the Russian folk-lore."

Modest was the youngest of four brothers, but the oldest two died when they were very young, leaving only Filaret who was three years older than he as a companion. Living on their father's vast estate, many miles from any city, they grew up without the companionship of other children. But what wonderful times they had together tumbling and sliding over the crisp white snow in winter and playing on the lake of their very own, called Shishitza, in summer!

Modest showed an early interest in the piano which made his father, who loved music, very happy. When Modest was scarcely more than a baby, his mother, whose name had been Julia Chirikova, gave him music lessons. She

3

was a sweet and gentle person who wrote poetry, played the piano, and in general, filled the Mussorgsky home with loveliness. But from the very first lesson, Modest displayed his own ideas in making music. Without the slightest idea of how or why he was striking a combination of notes, he made up music with remarkable effectiveness.

"He must have the best teachers," said Peter Mussorgsky.

"But that will have to wait," Modest's mother reminded her husband. "That will have to wait until we take the boys to St. Petersburg to put them in school."

Meanwhile she taught her young son to the best of her ability. And when he was seven he could sit down at the piano and play small pieces by Liszt with real distinction.

Modest was ten and his brother thirteen when their parents took them to St. Petersburg to put them in a preparatory school. Meanwhile Modest continued his music study. And one evening, when he was eleven, he astonished the guests in his father's home by playing a piano concerto by John Field—the brilliant Irish pianist and composer, known as the "Russian" Field—who had died at Moscow two years before Modest was born.

"That settles it!" declared Peter Mussorgsky. "Modest shall have a proper teacher."

Accordingly, the promising young musician was placed in the hands of one Anton Herke who was delighted with his pupil's progress. Within a year Modest played at a charity affair with sensational success and was happy indeed when Herke presented him with a copy of Beethoven's Sonata in A flat major as a fitting reward.

Soon it was time for another step in the boys' education. According to the custom in Russia at that time, they both entered the School of the Cadets of the Guards. And what a mistake this proved to be in the case of Modest! The harsh ways of a military school came as a terrible shock to a boy, studious and sensitive by nature, and only two years removed from a free, country life.

"Why, mother," he declared one day when he was permitted to visit his family, "the cadets consider study beneath them!"

4

"What an idea!" exclaimed Julia Chirikova Mussorgsky. "Whatever put that thought in your head?"

"It's true, mother. Honestly it is. Why, the other night when I was busy with my studies, the General appeared and began to make fun of me for studying so much, declaring, 'My dear boy, what kind of officer will you make!'"

Despite this rough atmosphere, it was during his first year at the School of the Cadets of the Guards that Modest's first musical composition was published. It was called *Ensign's Polka* and he dedicated it to his comrades in the school.

In later years Modest looked back to these school days with one grateful memory—to the teaching and companionship of the divinity master, Father Kroupsky. From him he gained a sound knowledge of old church music; and we can trace this influence in many of his compositions.

Then once more a family custom decided his fate, when at seventeen, he joined the famous Preobrajensky Regiment. But gradually music, his real interest, emerged from the routine of a military life. During that first year in the service, while visiting the military hospital, Modest met a young doctor who was as much interested in music as in medicine. His name was Alexander Borodin and he is famous today for his colorful opera *Prince Igor*. This meeting was the beginning of a long chain of musical friendships that eventually developed into a unit known as the "Mighty Handful" or "The Five."

During the same year young Mussorgsky was introduced to Alexander Sergeivitch Dargomyzhsky at whose home several young men often gathered for a musical evening. Dargomyzhsky was one of the leaders in a movement to create a genuine Russian form of music, and it is interesting to know that Mussorgsky eventually expressed in his music the aims of Dargomyzhsky which in his own words, were: "I wish the sound always to express the word in the most direct way. I aim at truth."

At one of these gatherings Mussorgsky met Cesar Cui, a young engineering officer, with whom Mussorgsky often played duets; and Mily Balakirev, a self-taught musician who later became Mussorgsky's teacher.

Balakirev, who as Borodin often said, gathered musicians about him "like a hen her chickens," was the founder of the "Russian Five." The original members were: Mily Balakirev, Cesar Cui, Alexander Borodin, Modest Mussorgsky and Nikolai Rimsky-Korsakov. But Vladimir Stassov, a critic, the only one who really understood Mussorgsky, was later associated with the group.

Mussorgsky became Balakirev's first real pupil in musical composition. Though benefited by his own study of Michail Glinka's operas, *A Life for the Tsar* and *Russlan and Ludmilla,* first examples of national Russian music, together with the study of Beethoven's symphonies, Balakirev had helped and advised many an aspiring young musician. Mussorgsky, as his pupil, gained in like-measure, but it was not long before Mussorgsky was expressing himself, musically, in ways unfamiliar even to Balakirev's original mind. And the world today must give a share of credit to Vladimir Stassov, who alone, understood and encouraged Mussorgsky to hold to his own ideas of composition.

In 1858, much against the advice of his friends, Mussorgsky resigned his commission in order to devote himself to composition. Not long afterward, he fell ill, and consequently spent some time at Glebove, a country estate of some wealthy friends.

The following year, when he was twenty years old, Mussorgsky visited Moscow for the first time. This event, in a way, brought him to himself. Let us see how he described this experience years later: "Moscow certainly transported me to another world, the world of the past—a world that, though it was full of horrors, still, I know not why, attracts me strongly. I will tell you something ... I believe that I am now beginning really to love my country." And anyone who hears his music today knows this to have been true, and listening, hears "Russia" in every note.

Mussorgsky did not find his own musical language overnight, but Alexander Borodin, after playing duets with him one evening, and then listening to Mussorgsky play something of his own, had this to say about it, "I was absolutely amazed at the strange new elements in his music."

Not long after this an event in Russian history directed the course in

Mussorgsky's life for a time. This was the Imperial Ukase in 1861, by which Tsar Alexander II freed the serfs of Russia, just as Lincoln's Proclamation, two years later, freed the slaves of the United States. Modest's father having died in 1855, his mother had been living in St. Petersburg, but this freeing of the serfs—a proper move in the eyes of Modest—lessened the family income. It was necessary for his mother to return to their estate at Karevo, where Modest's brother Filaret was living with his family. Mussorgsky soon joined her there to help his brother manage the estate.

During this period of helping in the business affairs of his family, Mussorgsky had little opportunity to write music; but one composition, *Intermezzo*, written first as a piano piece, and later scored or arranged for orchestra, had a picturesque beginning. During the winter of 1861 on a day bright with sunshine, Mussorgsky noticed a group of peasant boys walking over the snow-covered plains. With great difficulty they made their way through the drifts. Just so often some of them sank into the snow and then, with effort, pulled themselves out. "The effect," said Mussorgsky, "was charming and picturesque, gay and serious at the same time. Suddenly in the distance a crowd of young women appeared, singing and laughing as they came along the shining way. The picture at once took musical shape in my imagination; quite unexpectedly the first melody was born, with its vigorous up-and-down-Bach-like movement, and the merry, laughing women were transformed into the theme that I afterward used for the middle part . . . and that is how the *Intermezzo* came to be written."

Finally, Modest left all that remained of the family estate to his brother, explaining, "He is married and needs the money, I am capable of earning my own living." Thus it was, that he decided to go into the Civil Service by which means he earned his living off and on for eighteen years.

In 1863, having become a government clerk in the Engineering department of the Ministry of Transport, Modest settled in St. Petersburg with several other young men in a kind of "community" manner of living. This was the custom of the day and one which proved invigorating to young Mussorgsky. Each young man occupied a room of his own, but joined his friends at meals and in the evening to read or discuss matters of interest. In his

7

own words, Modest had begun to set his brains in order and to acquire much useful knowledge. Among those who visited this little "community" was Ivan Turgenev, the Russian novelist, whose writing greatly impressed young Mussorgsky.

Between the years 1864 and 1867 Mussorgsky composed some of his most characteristic music. In 1864 he wrote the powerful song, *Kallistrat* which sings the story of a ragged, peasant boy. Next came a beautiful song called *Night* and in 1865 appeared the lovely *Peasant's Lullaby*, dedicated to his mother who had just died.

Once again Mussorgsky fell ill and it became necessary for him to move from the "community" to his brother's home where he remained until the fall of 1868. During this time he wrote the songs, *Savishna* and *Hopak;* and a choral work, *The Rout of Sennacherib* which was performed under the direction of Balakirev at St. Petersburg in 1867; and the first draft of his only important orchestral work—now known as the *Night on the Bare Mountain.*

Mussorgsky dedicated this work to Balakirev, who unfortunately saw much to criticize in it, an attitude which hurt Mussorgsky exceedingly. He would not alter the work, however, and wrote to Balakirev: "But whether you agree to have it performed or not, I refuse to alter the form or the treatment, which correspond exactly to my views and feeling." And it was not performed during his lifetime, being fated to undergo vast revisions by Rimsky-Korsakov, after Mussorgsky's death, before it appeared in print.

Then Mussorgsky entered the most fruitful year of his life—that of 1868. In it, he wrote the first group of songs called *The Nursery;* set to music one act of Gogol's comedy *The Marriage;* and began his great opera, *Boris Godunov.*

In writing the songs that make up *The Nursery*, Mussorgsky went back in his memory to the happy childhood days with his nurse, and captured that spirit in music. This was the real Mussorgsky. No other composer would have revealed these vivid pictures of childhood in just the way he did, and in expressing *himself*, he created in each one of these songs a little masterpiece. This group of songs known as *The Nursery* eventually consisted of seven titles. They are: *With Nanny, Go Into the Corner, The Cockchafer, Dolly's Cradle Song, The Hobby-Horse, The Evening Prayer* and *The Cat and the Bird-Cage.* Mussorgsky wrote the words as well as the music to these dramatic scenes of childhood, and in each one suited the music exactly to that particular story.

At Triebschen on the Lake of Lucerne in Switzerland, another composer was also fitting words and music. This was Richard Wagner at work on the last act of *Siegfried,* the third, in his great cycle of four operas, *The Ring of the Nibelung.* Both composers were accused of departing too far afield from the accepted musical style, and both composers are honored today for that very thing. Each said in music what was in his heart and mind, and, in doing so, created something genuine.

Mussorgsky was now living with some friends by the name of Opochinin and this home—which became his for three years—proved to be both friendly and helpful to him. Throughout his life Mussorgsky had a tendency to be influenced by his surroundings. This was one of the good influences— one which made him both happy and creative.

He began the music of *The Marriage* in June of 1868 and finished the vocal part of the first act before a month had passed. In a letter that he wrote to Rimsky-Korsakov concerning this music we realize how simple and yet how exact were his intentions: "If I have managed to render the straight-forward expression of thoughts and feelings as it takes place in ordinary speech, and if my rendering is artistic and musicianly, then the deed is done."

And then again in his letter to Liudmila Shestakova, the Russian Composer Michail Glinka's sister, we read that same thought: "What I want to do is make my characters speak on the stage as they would in real life, and yet write music which will be thoroughly artistic."

He was groping his way in a direction that seemed too daring to his musician-friends, but his genius was about to come to full bloom in *Boris Godunov,* an opera which is today considered a masterpiece.

In the fall of this same eventful year of 1868, a friend, Professor Nikolsky, happened to be chatting with Mussorgsky. "Why don't you use Pushkin's tragedy *Boris Godunov* in an opera?" he asked.

"Splendid!" exclaimed Mussorgsky.

Work on *The Marriage* ceased instantly and *Boris Godunov* developed at such a pace that it was completed in December 1869. With a wonderful sense of accomplishment—of having succeeded in setting down in music a great tragedy—he submitted *Boris Godunov* to the management of the Imperial Opera.

Imagine his disappointment when they not only did not accept it, but did not understand what it was all about. Why! There was no part for a prima donna; there were no solos of any kind and no ballet! And because they were unfamiliar with this style of music it was all wrong.

There was nothing for him to do but make certain changes, changes which would satisfy the committee of the Imperial Opera and still not tamper with the spirit of his work. Accordingly, he put in more singing of the usual kind and added a whole act in which the hero and heroine were given a chance to sing a duet together. This revision took nearly two years during which time he shared a room with Rimsky-Korsakov who was then writing *The Maid of Pskov*. One writing table and one piano served them both— each taking his turn while the other went out on this duty or that.

Meanwhile Mussorgsky had been composing more songs, including: three belonging to *The Nursery*; one called *The Peep-Show* and another, *The Seminarist*. And then while the Imperial Opera committee was again trying to make up its mind about producing *Boris Godunov*, Mussorgsky fortunately found interest in a new work—*Khovanshchina*—suggested by his friend Stassov. Mussorgsky became thoroughly fascinated with the subject which was historical and Russian in character. To Stassov he wrote while in the midst of working out the libretto or story of the opera, "The goal of the artist should be to study the most subtle features of human beings and of humanity in the mass."

Absorbed in his new work, he did not suffer quite so keenly at the second rejection by the Imperial Opera of his *Boris Godunov*. But at this point, some of his friends took matters into their own hands and set about making plans to bring his opera before the public. They managed to have three scenes from *Boris* performed, with great success, on February 5, 1873, on

10

the stage of the Imperial Opera at a benefit performance. Plans were made for more such performances and a music publisher bought the rights; but still the opera, as a whole, remained unproduced.

And that summer was a very unhappy one for Mussorgsky. In addition to his disappointment in regard to the opera, he was deeply affected by the death of his friend, a young painter-architect by the name of Victor Hartmann. It was, in fact, from an exhibit of this young man's sketches and paintings, shortly afterward, that Mussorgsky drew the inspiration for his set of piano pieces called *Pictures From an Exhibition*. Today we are more familiar with the orchestral version, arranged by the French composer, Maurice Ravel. In it the music begins with a "Promenade" in which we can truly see in sound a visitor walk into a picture gallery, look about to get his bearings, and then after a moment of uncertainty saunter towards a picture called "Gnomes." Once more the "Promenade" music appears, as the visitor moves on to another picture—this time "The Old Castle." Thus the music carries us on until we have looked in sound with the imaginary gallery visitor at ten different pictures, ending with the one called "The Great Gate at Kiev."

The autumn of 1873 brought better prospects for a *Boris Godunov* production when Julia Platonova who had taken part in the benefit performance, insisted that the complete opera be given for her benefit—a benefit performance being due her at that time. Thus it was that *Boris Godunov* was produced for the first time on January 27, 1874, at the Imperial Opera. The audience was very much impressed, but the critics, with the exception of Stassov, were boldly critical. Rimsky-Korsakov praised it for its originality but hated it for what he considered its clumsiness.

Twenty-six performances of the opera were given, however, from that time until 1881. Then it was withdrawn until long after Mussorgsky's death.

Greatly depressed and in poor health, Mussorgsky withdrew from most of his friends, with the exception of Stassov and the poet, Golenistchev-Koutouzov, with whom he lived from 1873 to 1875. The latter wrote the words to two sets of songs composed by Mussorgsky. These are called *Songs and Dances of Death* and *Sunless;* and are indeed wonderful songs.

11

Sunless consists of six songs in which Mussorgsky created both in the musical accompaniment and in the melodies themselves a definite feeling of what the poet intended in the words. Later, Claude Debussy, the French composer, captured in like-manner a mood or spirit in his music. The four songs making up the *Songs and Dances of Death* group are intensely dramatic in nature. The best known one, *Trepak, Death and the Peasant*, takes its name from the principal theme of the song—a trepak which is a national dance. The story, of a dying peasant as he lies dreaming within a deep forest amid wind and snow, is exactly told in the music, ending with the return of the trepak theme which breaks in to the peasant's dream— "echoing far away...".

In 1875 Mussorgsky went to live with another friend, Paul Naoumov, who was not one of the "good" influences in his life. Mussorgsky's health was failing, and a regulated way of life would have been of great benefit. In spite of these unfavorable conditions, however, he was working on two operas at the same time: one based on Gogol's Ukranian story, *The Sorochintsi Fair* and the one called *Khovanschina*.

Then to the horror of his friends, Mussorgsky went on a tour as accompanist to Daria Leonova, one of the singers of *Boris Godunov*. But he thoroughly enjoyed this trip through southern Russia—the farthest he ever traveled from St. Petersburg. On his return, having left the government service, he once again shocked his friends by accepting a position of accompanist and advisor to the same singer's vocal classes.

At the beginning of the new year, two groups of friends gave him, independent of each other, monthly allowances: one, that he might finish *Khovanschina* and the other that he might finish *The Sorochintsi Fair*.

We can picture poor Mussorgsky, broken in health, but honestly and conscientiously working away on both operas at the same time. Alas! He was to finish neither one. On February 12, 1881, he fell seriously ill, and was taken to a hospital where for a time it seemed that he might recover, but paralysis set in and he died on March 28, 1881.

He was buried in the famous Alexander Nevsky Cemetery near the tomb of his forerunner, Michail Glinka; and then his friends set about preparing

12

his music for publication. The result was one of the most unusual in musical history. Some unkind fate still hovered over Mussorgsky; for he who had striven always to be himself in music was destined to be represented for nearly fifty years in greatly edited and changed versions of his works.

"With whatever shortcomings my music is born, with them it must live if at all," Mussorgsky once wrote to Rimsky-Korsakov, but Rimsky-Korsakov honestly believed that the beauty of *Boris Godunov* and much of Mussorgsky's other music would benefit by polishing. And in the polished form, the world has known Mussorgsky's music. It was not until 1928 that the original version of *Boris Godunov* was given at the Marinsky Theatre at Leningrad which was called St. Petersburg in Mussorgsky's day.

Now that Mussorgsky's original scores are available in a special edition, edited by Paul Lamm, we can at last judge his music on its own merits, as Mussorgsky insisted. And the genuine Mussorgsky is unlike any other composer: realist, but not a musical picture-painter; nationalist, but not a musical flag-waver. By birth a Russian, by nature a lover of humanity, and endowed with a sensitive gift for musical expression, Mussorgsky emerges today the genuine Russian composer.

DVOŘÁK

ANTONIN DVOŘÁK

Voice of Bohemia

BORN 1841—DIED 1904

Antonin Dvořák was born on September 8, 1841 at Nelahozeves, known also by its German name Mühlhausen, in Bohemia. Bohemia, a sturdy little Slavic country—set for three centuries like a glowing jewel in the midst of the Austrian Empire—suddenly burst forth in the middle of the nineteenth century with a national music. And Antonin Dvořák was destined to become her most famous musical son.

Bohemians, later known as Czecho-Slovakians, had always sung and danced among themselves, but it was not until about the time that Antonin Dvořák was reaching manhood that Bohemia—like so many of her neighbors including Russia—suddenly became aware of her own musical nationality.

Little Antonin, whose father, František Dvořák, was an innkeeper and a butcher, was the eldest of eight children. And although František Dvořák played the zither and sang songs to the delight of his patrons who visited his inn on the River Moldau, and although he encouraged his young son to study music with Josef Spitz, the village schoolmaster—who could play any instrument—he had no intention of Antonin's becoming a musician. It was the natural thing for a Bohemian youth to learn to play and sing, but he must also make his living. And to this end, Antonin's father insisted that his son learn the butcher's trade.

At this point good fortune stepped into the picture. A childless uncle, living at Zlonice, forty-five miles west of the city of Prague, invited Antonin there to continue his musical education. And this proved to be a favorable turn of events. There was an exceptional schoolmaster and organist by the name of Anton Liehmann at Zlonice with whom Antonin studied organ, piano, the viola, musical theory and German. Surely a great deal for one man to teach, or one pupil to learn! Liehmann was greatly impressed with young Antonin's talents and urged the boy's father to send him to Prague for further study.

Alas, business matters were no better for František Dvořák, who meanwhile had transferred his shop to Zlonice. It was simply out of the question for him to send Antonin to Prague to study. The best that could be managed was an exchange arrangement whereby a young German boy came to Zlonice to learn the Bohemian language while Antonin went to the town of Bohmisch-Kamnitz for a year to perfect his German.

At the end of that time there was no choice in the matter. His father needed him in the shop, and since there was no money to make his Prague dreams possible, Antonin, at fifteen, found himself a shop-keeper's assistant.

But at this time in addition to playing various musical instruments, he began to compose. With great pride he rehearsed, with some friends, a polka which he had written and completely scored himself as both a surprise and a challenge to his father. Two mistakes contrived to make the result funny instead of fruitful. First of all, he did not know that the trumpet was a transposing instrument, that when you wrote a certain note it was going to *play* another. In the second place, he did not bother to rehearse the full score. Consequently, when bursting with pride he appeared before his father with his little band of players, the trumpet players, blowing forth the notes as they were written, played in an entirely different key from the rest of the musicians. And poor Antonin had to agree when his father declared, "It doesn't make any sense!"

In spite of this inauspicious beginning as a composer, Antonin with the continued encouragement from his teacher Anton Liehmann and the help of his kind uncle, gained permission from his father to go to Prague. He traveled there in a hay-cart and his black eyes danced with excitement at the first sight of the famous city. Exactly thirty years before, another young boy—who was destined to become a great composer—Richard Wagner, then thirteen years old had gazed with equal fascination on this same scene. He had been overcome at the picturesque beauty of Prague, just as young Dvořák was on this day when the city sparkled there in the sunlight.

Antonin enrolled at once in the Organ School and became a very busy young man. He took organ lessons at the Cathedral; studied the orchestra in the Cecelia Society and played the viola on many occasions to help maintain himself. His father gave him a small allowance for a short time, but it was scarcely enough to pay for the necessities of life. Consequently, anything extra for concert or opera tickets had to be earned. The story goes, however, that young Dvořák managed to hear many an opera—without benefit of ticket—by slipping unnoticed into the orchestra pit and hiding behind the drums!

Then the friendship of a young composer, Karl Bendl, brought an important new influence into his life. Bendl, who had previously studied at the Organ School and had later gone to Amsterdam, was now back in his own country, eager to be a part of the growing Bohemian nationalism. Bendl lent Dvořák scores that opened an entirely new world, and when Dvořák was graduated from the Organ School, Bendl was responsible for his being taken into the orchestra of the National Opera as a viola-player.

Still another person, Joseph Foerster, one of Dvořák's teachers, proved important in his musical growth. Foerster had been professor of musical theory at the Prague Conservatory and was later organist of the Prague Cathedral: Dvořák benefited particularly from Foerster's great admiration for Palestrina's music.

Meanwhile Dvořák had begun to compose—chamber music and then symphonies: the first symphony being called *The Bells of Zlonice* in honor of his uncle's town. And for several years he continued to play in the orchestra, to give private music lessons and to compose a vast amount of music much of which he destroyed.

Then Bedrich Smetana, known as the "Father of Bohemian Music" and famous today for his opera *The Bartered Bride*, came home from Sweden to act as conductor of the opera. He took a friendly interest in Dvořák

19

and helped to direct the ambitious young composer away from the classic, German style of music into a natural spontaneous expression of his own people.

After having tried his hand, quite unsuccessfully, at an opera called *Alfred*, written much in the style of Richard Wagner with reoccurring motives or themes, Dvořák wrote *King and Collier*, a humorous opera, which was eventually produced in a revised form with a good bit of success. He was beginning to find himself, but it was not until 1873 with his patriotic hymn —*The Heirs of the White Mountain*—that Dvořák really came into his own. This was a hymn of praise, written for a mixed chorus and orchestra, to honor the memory of the brave defenders of Bohemia in 1620 at the Battle of the White Mountain. It was performed on March 9th of the year 1873, and brought immediate recognition to Dvořák.

Still another happiness came that year in his marriage to Anna Cermakova, one of his pupils. And we can truly say, as they do in the fairy tales, "They lived happily ever after." Music was now flowing from him with no apparent effort: chamber music, a symphony and an opera *The Pig-headed Peasants*.

Then in 1875 he was awarded a grant from the Austrian Government. He had submitted a symphony and other compositions in the state competition, and none other than Johannes Brahms—the famous German composer who lived a great part of his life in Vienna—was on the committee. Brahms became a true champion of Dvořák's music, and was eventually responsible for the first publication of his music.

Hans von Bülow, noted pianist and conductor, also became a good friend. And it was to him that Dvořák dedicated his Symphony in F. For another admirer—Joseph Joachim, the famous violinist—Dvořák wrote a concerto. And to Hans Richter—the noted conductor who at the beginning of his career as a young horn-player had helped in the writing-down of Wagner's comic opera *The Mastersingers*—Dvořák dedicated his Symphony in D.

Gradually Dvořák's fame spread. The first of his *Slavonic Dances* were published in 1878 as piano duets. More and more conductors and artists were playing his music in various European cities. And then in 1884 came an invitation to conduct his *Stabat Mater* in London. He had written this—

prompted largely by the death of his daughter—in a period of six weeks. The original *Stabat Mater* is part of the Catholic church musical service, used on special days of the year, but various composers including Palestrina, Haydn, Schubert, Rossini and Verdi as well as Dvořák have made their own settings, or versions, of it.

Dvořák conducted his *Stabat Mater* at Albert Hall in London with such success that he was invited to return to England in the fall to conduct it at the Worcester Festival. He was then commissioned to write a new work— the cantata, *The Spectre's Bride*—for the Birmingham Festival. And in the year 1886 he once again visited England: this time to conduct his oratorio, *St. Ludmila* at the Leeds Festival. But he was, unfortunately, influenced in this composition by the English love of Handel's *Messiah* and Mendelssohn's *Elijah*. The result was not a happy one. Realizing that this style of music was not suited to his spontaneous Bohemian nature—just as he had dis- covered early in his career that Wagner's way of writing operas was not his way—Dvořák never again strayed into musical paths, foreign to his own nature.

Meanwhile he had bought a country place in southern Bohemia, where, a portion of each year, he raised pigeons, wrote music to his heart's content and enjoyed the company of the peasants and miners in the community.

Honors poured in upon him from many directions. He was appointed Professor of Composition at the Prague Conservatory; Cambridge Univer- sity in England made him an honorary Musical Doctor; the Czech Uni- versity in Prague granted him a degree of Doctor of Philosophy; he was decorated by the Austrian Government and eventually made a life-member of the Austrian House of Lords.

Meanwhile out of a clear blue sky, shortly before his fiftieth birthday, Dvořák was invited to go to America as director of the National Conserva- tory in New York City. The Conservatory had been founded in 1885 by Mrs. Jeanette Thurber, a wealthy music-lover, who now felt that Dvořák's name would add prestige to the institution which she hoped might one day rival the famous Paris Conservatoire.

New York looked a long way from home to Dvořák and his family as they pored over a map of the world together, but a salary of fifteen thousand dollars a year was too tempting to resist. Think of all the splendid things they could do with that much money! And so with a leave of absence arranged with the Prague Conservatory, and many farewell concerts ringing in their ears, Dvořák, his wife, their six children and three other members of their household set out for America.

New York greeted Dvořák with a great concert in which the Metropolitan Orchestra of eighty and a chorus of three hundred took part. The singing of *America* was included in the program and Dvořák's cycle of three overtures called *Nature, Life, Love* was given its first American performance. After a speech of welcome Dvořák was presented with a silver wreath; and he was indeed made to feel welcome in this American city. But only Bohemia was *home* to Dvořák, and try as he might to avoid it—throughout his three years' stay in America—his mind continually wandered homeward.

Dvořák was not a trained teacher, but his colorful personality and originality of expression gave a kind of character to the newly-organized Conservatory. And among the American composers who benefited by his teaching was Harry Rowe Shelley, noted organist and composer of church music.

Harry Rowe Shelley always remembered certain dramatic incidents connected with his Bohemian teacher: for instance, when a pupil showed Dvořák a composition in which he had used twelve trumpets, Dvořák, looking thoughtfully at the score, remarked: "It's all right if you have something for them to say. But two were enough for Beethoven!" And another time, Shelley having labored long and lovingly on a symphony, had searched New York City for the finest possible manuscript paper to clothe his creation. With bursting pride, mingled with uncertainty, he presented Dvořák with his precious score. Dvořák, sitting at his desk, scanned one page after another, with, what Shelley considered, rapt interest. Then, glancing up at his eager pupil, and rubbing the edges of the manuscript between his fingers, Dvořák remarked, "Good paper. Where do you buy it?" And once again, having looked at one of Shelley's scores, he made certain corrections and then remarked: "I'm glad you did that. Now, go put it away in a drawer. You won't make that mistake again."

22

Dvořák, in turn, learned about America from his students; and thus inspired, set about writing his famous symphony, *From the New World*. After putting down the last notes of the first draft of this symphony, Dvořák went with his whole family to Spillville, Iowa, for a summer vacation. What a wonderful time they had in this Bohemian community—set down in the middle of the United States—eleven miles from a railway station!

"Why! It is just like home!" the children cried.

Dvořák played on the village organ; his wife sang in the choir; his children ran and played to their heart's content; and Dvořák wrote music when he felt like it and sometimes he just sat! Hearing a bird sing merrily away, inspired the third movement of his "Nigger" quartet; and before he had scarcely finished the work, it was being rehearsed and played by a quartet of players, made up of the village schoolmaster, his children, and Dvořák.

Then came a wonderful celebration for Dvořák's fifty-second birthday, with music, speeches, decorations, and a feast. Surely this was just like Bohemia. And to top off the honors bestowed upon him, Iowa later named a road "The Dvořák Highway" and marked it with a memorial tablet bearing his name.

Returning to New York by way of Niagara Falls, Dvořák once more took up his Conservatory duties. Then on December 15, 1893, his *From the New World* symphony was played at Carnegie Hall under Anton Seidl with great success. In addition to this famous work, and the "Nigger" quartet, he composed among other things, while in America, his violin sonatina, written for his children, the splendid violoncello concerto, and some of the famous piano pieces, *Humoresques*.

When the time arrived to renew his contract with the Conservatory, Dvořák's home-sickness for Bohemia won the day. In the spring of 1895 the Dvořák family sailed for home with the thought that Dvořák would return to America in 1897. This plan never materialized. Instead, he continued to live a very busy life in Bohemia with his teaching at the Prague Conservatory and much composing. During this last period of his career he wrote three operas and many symphonic poems, or music with stories. Among these

23

were: *The Watersprite, The Midday Witch, The Golden Spinning Wheel, The Wood Dove,* and *Heroic Song.*

In 1901 Bohemia gave her illustrious son a great festival for his sixtieth birthday, and Dvořák looked forward to many years of creative work. His hope was not to be realized, for he died quite unexpectedly at dinner on May 1, 1904. The whole nation mourned his death and buried him with great sorrow on May the fifth.

Dvořák, whose name immediately brings to mind his famous *Songs My Mother Taught Me* or *From the New World* symphony, possessed a natural gift for melody, a feeling for rhythm and a love of his country—all of which bubbled forth with unrestrained emotion in his music. Even when we listen to his *From the New World* symphony—supposed to be "America"—we distinctly hear "Bohemia."

RIMSKY - KORSAKOV

Courtesy of "Musical Courier"

NIKOLAI ANDREYEVITCH RIMSKY-KORSAKOV

Master of Orchestral Color

BORN 1844—DIED 1908

Nikolai ANDREYEVITCH RIMSKY-KORSAKOV—destined to be the most famous of the "Russian Five," or the "Mighty Handful"—was born on March 18, 1844, in Russia at Tichvin in the Government of Novgorod. Modest Mussorgsky was five years old and Peter Ilyitch Tchaikovsky a year younger.

Nikolai grew up in a large and comfortable house situated at the edge of town on the bank of the Tichvinka River opposite the Tichvin Monastery. The Rimsky-Korsakov home consisted of Nikolai, his father, who had retired from Government service, his mother, and Uncle Peter, or "Uncle Pipon," his father's elder brother. Nikolai's only brother, Voin Nikolayevitch, was away from home, serving as a naval lieutenant; and true to family tradition, Nikolai looked upon all to do with ships and water with favor. In due time he, too, would become a naval officer!

Meanwhile he had a jolly time playing games mostly of his own invention; on many an occasion he would pile high a rocking chair with a variety of possessions, clamber into the midst of them and pretend for hours that the chair was either his castle or a wonderful ship sailing off to sea.

Then in the evenings friends and family often gathered in the Rimsky-Korsakov home to play and sing. Nikolai's father would play the piano by ear and both his mother and "Uncle Pipon" would sing folk-songs by the hour: some of which found their way into a famous collection of folk-songs gathered by Rimsky-Korsakov many years later.

Before little Nikolai was two years old he astonished his family by calling off the names of the songs as his mother sang them; and by the time he was three or four he became an "orchestra" player: that is, in his own family! For no matter how quickly his father would change the rhythm in a piece, Nikolai followed along by tapping out the time on his little drum. Soon he could sing the songs his father played; then he could pick out the tunes with his own harmonies on the piano; and finally, having learned the names of the notes, he could stand in another room and call their names as they were struck on the piano.

When he was six years old he began to take music lessons from an elderly neighbor—Yekatyerina Nikolayevna Unkovskaya—who guided him in playing scales, exercises, and a few simple pieces. He learned to read music with no effort, but he did not apply himself with any enthusiasm. Then after about two years of this indifferent study he was turned over to a more experienced teacher, a governess in the Fel family, friends of the Rimsky-Korsakovs'. Under her guidance he made more progress; and he remembered in later years that he especially liked a Beethoven sonata which he played as a duet with her.

At the end of a year or so, Olga Fyeliksovna Fel, pupil of this same governess, took him in hand and with her he continued his music study for about three years. During this time he made the acquaintance of a song and a duet from Michail Ivanovitch Glinka's opera *A Life for the Tsar*. Deeply moved by this music—whose creator is known as the "Father of Russian Music"—Nikolai immediately set about, in secret, to compose a duet of his own; then an "overture" for piano, in a completely original pattern.

In addition to the music which was a part of the Rimsky-Korsakov home and these informal music lessons, there was one other early musical experience that played an important part in Nikolai's later life: this was the singing and colorful service at the Tichvin Monastery to which "Uncle Pipon" often took him.

But now he was twelve years old and the time had come to leave these familiar surroundings. And since he had been away from Tichvin only three times in his entire life, the prospect of going to St. Petersburg to

28

study was both thrilling and frightening. For in spite of Voin's attempts to keep his young brother out of—what he considered—the bad company of the naval officers, Nikolai insisted upon training for the Imperial Navy.

Accordingly, in July 1856, he was taken by his father to St. Petersburg and duly entered in the Naval College where he became—in a twinkling of an eye—*Cadet* Rimsky-Korsakov!

Fortunately he was not entirely alone in this strange new world, for he was made to feel part of the family in the home of one P. N. Golovin—a friend of his brother's—where he spent every Saturday and Sunday. This served as a welcome change from the routine of the Naval Corps where Nikolai, at first, found the rigid discipline trying. Soon he made himself popular, however, with his classmates by holding his own with upper class tormentors; and his days began to fall into a friendly pattern.

During this first year at school, music occupied very little of his time although he did take piano lessons on Sundays while at the Golovins' from a 'cellist by the name of Ulich.

And then—it was time to go home for the summer holiday. What a relief to be home and free!

He returned to school in the fall with real regret and for some time showed little of the good behavior of the previous year. His weekends with the Golovins continued, and twice during the season he went with them to the opera where he heard, on one occasion, Flotow's *Indra* and, on another, *Lucia di Lammermoor*. The latter stirred his interest in music again and he found himself whistling the melodies, picking out parts on the piano, and even making notes after the performance.

That summer, Nikolai's brother Voin, having returned from a long sea voyage, was made commander of a target practice ship called Prokhov. And to Nikolai's great delight, Voin took him on the ship for the summer. All went well until one day while—according to his brother's plan—Nikolai was learning the "feel" of the ship, he tumbled out of the rigging into the sea!—Fortunately it was the *sea* and not the *deck,* for once he was hauled out of the water by the frightened sailors, he was found to be unhurt except for a slight bump where he had hit the water.

The following school year passed without any momentous happening except for his increased musical experience in the company of the Golovins. During this season he heard many more operas, including: Meyerbeer's *Robert le Diable* which pleased him greatly, Weber's *Der Freischutz*, and most important of all—Glinka's *A Life For the Tsar*. These operas introduced him into the wonderful world of the orchestra—and although he did not know the word, let alone its meaning, he had an immediate feeling for orchestration. Then when at his insistence, the Golovins unearthed some selections from Glinka's other great opera, *Russlan and Ludmilla*, he was indeed excited. Later in his memoirs he recalled this experience, remembering that he felt the beauty of *harmony* for the first time.

Meanwhile he had begun to take lessons from a good pianist, F. A. Canille, who, to Nikolai's delight, greatly admired Glinka's music and, in fact, considered *Russlan and Ludmilla* the best opera in the world. Canille, being a fine musician, introduced his young pupil to much other good music, including Bach's fugues and Beethoven's sonatas; and also encouraged him to compose. But in spite of these qualifications, Canille was no teacher.

Consequently, Nikolai, at sixteen—though liking music, and obviously talented—did not know the first thing about the theory or structure of music. Referring to this period in later years he wrote regretfully: "At that time nobody had taught me anything, nobody had guided my steps. And it would have been so simple, if only there had been the person to do it!"

Those who became *his* pupils, evidently benefited by this experience for many years later, one of them made this statement, "Rimsky-Korsakov was the most wonderful teacher in the world."

At the end of a year Voin decided that the music lessons should stop and Nikolai, although disappointed, accepted the decision. Canille, however, invited him to come to his house on Sundays to play duets and talk music. Meanwhile young Rimsky-Korsakov organized a choir of eighteen musically-minded Cadets which he successfully conducted, until, for some reason, the naval authorities frowned upon the venture.

Fate intended, however, that music should win over the sea, for in the

30

late fall of 1861 Canille introduced Rimsky-Korsakov to Mily Balakirev, and this meeting set aflame a fire already smoldering within the young cadet. Balakirev was the leader of Russia's musical awakening; for unlike her neighboring country, Germany, where music schools and technical training were readily available, Russia had had no musical conservatories.

Balakirev, a natural born musician with an exceptional bright mind and sparkling personality, had gathered about him a group of young men who were destined to make musical history. Now Rimsky-Korsakov—at seventeen—became a regular Saturday night visitor at Balakirev's home where he met Modest Mussorgsky, then twenty-two years old and already the composer of some music that had been played in public; Cesar Cui who had written an opera; Vladimir Stassov a noted critic; and others who were *doing* things. What a thrilling experience for the young naval cadet! And how he drank in the music-talk and serious discussion!

Then best of all when he showed Balakirev some of his own music, including fragments of a symphony, Balakirev was favorably impressed and insisted that Rimsky-Korsakov finish it. No matter that Russia had never produced a symphony; that neither Balakirev nor Rimsky-Korsakov knew anything about writing a symphony: it was obvious from his fragmentary selections, that Rimsky-Korsakov had a feeling for symphonic music. All he need do was go ahead and write it. And that is exactly what he set about to do!

Balakirev's favorite pupil whose name was Gusakovsky had just left the inner circle for distant lands. Consequently, not being overly hopeful of either Mussorgsky or Cui, Balakirev welcomed Rimsky-Korsakov with open arms. "I put my trust in you," he wrote to Rimsky-Korsakov on one occasion. And his trust was well founded, for Rimsky-Korsakov finished the first movement of his symphony within a month, and set about at once to orchestrate it with Balakirev's help. They all marveled at his instinctive use of instruments just as we do today.

In March of 1862 Rimsky-Korsakov was well into the last movement of his symphony when he was called to Tichvin by the serious illness of his father who died at the age of seventy-eight and was buried at the Greater

Monastery at Tichvin. Since January of that year Voin had been director of the Marine Corps. Now Madame Rimsky-Korsakov and "Uncle Pipon" went to live with Voin in St. Petersburg and Nikolai began to spend his Sundays with them.

In April of 1862 Nikolai was graduated as a midshipman which meant nothing at all until he had undergone some practical training when he would be examined for entrance into the official kingdom of the Navy. Meanwhile although Balakirev fought desperately to keep his young disciple at work on his music, Cui, as a government official himself, advised Rimsky-Korsakov: "You are young. Go ahead and get your commission. In a few years you will know better what you want to do."

And Voin, who saw no signs of unusual talent in either his young brother's piano playing or in his compositions, put his foot down and declared: "Get your commission!"

Thus it was that in the fall of 1862, Nikolai Rimsky-Korsakov set sail for three years' cruise on the "Almaz." They went first to England where they were obliged to stay for nearly four months while their ship was being re-rigged at Gravesend. During that time Rimsky-Korsakov made two trips to London with some of his naval companions. They visited Westminster Abbey, and many other famous places; and upon one occasion, attended the opera at Covent Garden. The Royal Italian Opera was playing there at the time, but in recalling the experience in later years, Rimsky-Korsakov could not remember what opera he had heard.

Meanwhile during his enforced leisure he had many political discussions with the other midshipmen. One of them bought several books, including John Stuart Mill's *On Liberty* and they all read and discussed the famous social weekly, "The Bell," published by the Russian exile, Alexander Herzen. It was a period of great liberation: the serfs were being freed in Russia, the struggle was going on towards liberating the slaves in the United States, and all over the world when young men gathered together they discussed the New Freedom.

In spite of political and maritime interruptions, Rimsky-Korsakov did not entirely neglect his music. Heeding Balakirev's pleading by letter, he continued to work on his symphony and since there was no piano aboard the ship, many a public house in England can lay claim to having had bits of Russia's first symphony—while in the making—played on its piano.

The "Almaz" having been repaired, she was ordered back into Baltic waters due to the Polish-Rebel situation. And while she was anchored at Kronstadt, Rimsky-Korsakov visited St. Petersburg. Then suddenly, because of the threat of war with England the "Almaz" was secretly ordered to set sail for the United States where she might help interfere with English-American shipping.

The trip by the northern route took nearly two months and then in October of 1863 the "Almaz" arrived in American waters. Joining a squadron of Russian ships, she cruised along the Atlantic Coast until April of the following year. During this time—while the United States was in the midst of the Civil War—Rimsky-Korsakov and his companions made excursions to Baltimore, Washington, New York, and other American cities; and even took a memorable trip to Niagara Falls where the power and the beauty of this magnificent water-drama made a lasting impression on the young seaman. The majesty of sound and orchestral color fired his eager imagination and stored away tones that came to life later in his music.

On a trip to New York he attended the opera where he heard Gounod's *Faust* and Meyerbeer's *Robert le Diable*. Picture him returning to "Almaz," and picking out the opera airs and American tunes on the cabin harmonium while another member of the crew played the fiddle!

The correspondence with Balakirev had practically ceased, and now Rimsky-Korsakov had become enough of a sailor to have pushed aside the thought of becoming a serious musician. He was thoroughly enjoying himself in spite of his distaste for brutal naval discipline. And when the danger of war with England being over, the "Almaz" was ordered home by way of Cape Horn and the Pacific, Rimsky-Korsakov was happy indeed. Why! He would see the whole world!

But alas! The captain of the "Almaz" did not share this enthusiasm for travel. While Gendemarine Rimsky-Korsakov—on their trip down the American coast—was marveling over the phosphorescent gleams of stars and water, Captain Zelaney was contriving ways and means to avoid the Pacific crossing. After taking about sixty-five days to sail from New York to Rio de Janeiro, he changed the power from sail to steam and then proceeded to break down the engines, making it necessary to return to Rio de Janeiro for repairs. Then having sent to Russia an exaggerated account of his ship's plight, he settled down with his crew at Rio to await orders.

In October came the reply, "Return at once to Europe."

Thus it was that "Almaz" changed her course, and young Rimsky-Korsakov had occasion to visit Nice, Marseilles and other southern European ports.

Back at Kronstadt, at the beginning of 1865, Rimsky-Korsakov—now a midshipman—found both friends and family away in the country. He saw Balakirev a few times while waiting for the "Almaz" to be dismantled, but he was now more officer-dilettante, or dabbler, than creative musician.

September found him stationed in St. Petersburg where he gradually picked up the threads of his musical life. While he had been roaming the seas the Russian musical family—under Balakirev's guidance—had grown both in size and importance. Alexander Borodin, a young chemical professor from the Medical Academy, was at work on a symphony; the Free School, founded by Balakirev in 1862, had become a flourishing institution and now before Rimsky-Korsakov realized what was happening he was in the midst of finishing his own first symphony!

Meanwhile he wrote his first song to words by the German poet, Heine. Balakirev, approving of the melody though not the accompaniment, proceeded to write an accompaniment himself and the song was eventually published in that form.

But the chief interest of the fall centered in the symphony. Finished without benefit of formal musical training, it was given its first performance —after two rehearsals—on one of the Free School concerts. Thus it was that Rimsky-Korsakov's and Russia's first symphony saw the light of day at the end of December in 1865 in the company of Mozart's *Requiem*. The audience was pleased with the music and thoroughly astonished when a young naval officer appeared to acknowledge the applause.

That winter he became a regular visitor at the home of Liudmila Shestakova where he met the composer, Alexander Dargomyzhsky and a singer by the name of Zotova. For her he composed the famous song *The Rose Enslaves the Nightingale*, and two other songs, all of which were published together with the first Heine song that had been "polished" by Balakirev. Not a coin did he receive for them but he had the wonderful satisfaction of seeing his songs in print!

Meanwhile Balakirev, having buried himself in the harmonizing of folksongs, brought back from a trip to the Caucasus, now attracted Rimsky-Korsakov's attention to this music. The immediate result was an orchestral piece called *Overture On Three Russian Themes*. Still unschooled in the use of musical instruments, Rimsky-Korsakov, nevertheless, did creditably with the help of Hector Berlioz's title *Treatise on Instrumentation*—a work which has remained useful both in its original form and in the edition augmented by Richard Strauss.

Once again Rimsky-Korsakov kept musical company dear to his heart when his "Russian" Overture was given in December 1866, at a Free School concert, together with Franz Liszt's *Mephisto Waltz*.

The young naval-composer was now leading a double life in this way: Balakirev, admiring Mussorgsky's skill as a pianist, had little patience with Rimsky-Korsakov's piano playing; Rimsky-Korsakov determined to improve his piano technique! Within him there was a deep-seated urge to learn— a quality that consistently contributed to his doing a good job. He worked like a bee—as has many another student—at Czerny's "Daily Exercises" and struggled gallantly through Chopin's Etudes: the result being, that he wholly delighted his naval companions with his piano playing and was considered quite the *pianist* at his brother Voin's home.

Notwithstanding, his musical family continued to recognize and encourage his talent for orchestration. The year 1867 found him started on a second symphony. This was never finished though some of it was used in another work. He hurriedly wrote a *Fantasia on Serbian Themes* which was played in the spring on Balakirev's Pan-Slavonic Concert. And then in the beginning of June he began—what is sometimes regarded as Russia's first symphonic poem—*Sadko*. This was finished in the early fall. To Mussorgsky with whom

35

he had now become more intimate, Rimsky-Korsakov announced that *Sadko* was by far the best thing he had done. And frankly admitting the influence of Liszt, Glinka, Dargomyzhsky, and even his mentor, Balakirev, Rimsky-Korsakov later expressed an opinion that *Sadko* possessed an original form and a freshness of treatment, writing, "the orchestral color scheme miraculously caught, despite my ignorance of orchestration."

Hector Berlioz, whose treatise on instrumentation Rimsky-Korsakov so diligently followed, came that fall as guest conductor of the Russian Musical Society. Balakirev, the Society's permanent conductor that season, had engineered this visit, but strangely enough—due to Berlioz's ill health or to his lack of interest in budding young Russian composers—none of the "Five" except Balakirev and Cui met the vitriolic French composer whose orchestral mantle Rimsky-Korsakov was destined to inherit.

Balakirev conducted *Sadko* at its first performance together with the *Serbian Fantasia* on a Russian Music Society program in December of 1867. Both were immensely successful with the audience. Rimsky-Korsakov, the composer, was on his way!

During this time Rimsky-Korsakov had been living—or shall we say sleeping—in a furnished room on Vassily Island. He took his meals in his brother's home and spent most of his evenings with one or another of the musical brotherhood. In the spring of 1868 the entire group began to meet once a week at Dargomyzhsky's home where the host was at the fever-pitch stage of composing his opera *The Stone Guest,* based on the play of the same name by the great Russian poet, Alexander Pushkin. This was an exciting experience for all of them. As each fragment of the opera was finished it was immediately performed by the circle to whose number had been added the talented young sisters Alexandra and Nadejda Purgold. Alexandra was a singer, and Nadejda—who was destined to become Madame Rimsky-Korsakov—was a trained pianist. Later, the "circle" often visited the Purgold home where the singing, four-hand playing and musical talk went on into the wee hours of the morning.

But Rimsky-Korsakov was not neglecting his own work. At the beginning of the year 1868 he had started a symphonic poem—or suite as he afterward called it—based on an oriental tale—*Antar*. And buzzing about in his head was a plan for an opera based on a play called *The Maid of Pskov*. Despite the fact that Balakirev, together with Mussorgsky, had had a hand in suggesting both of these subjects, it was during his work on *Antar* that Rimsky-Korsakov began to break away from Balakirev's influence and to stand on his own feet as a composer.

Left alone in St. Petersburg, with the exception of Cui and Dargomyzhsky that summer, Rimsky-Korsakov, while living in his brother's naval college quarters, progressed with *Antar* and occasionally made excursions into the country to visit the Purgold family. With tactful impartiality he wrote two songs—*Night* and *Secret:* the first for Nadejda Purgold and the latter for her sister Alexandra.

Then in July came an invitation to visit the Lodyjenskys' estate in the interior of Russia where the Borodins were spending the summer. As he sat in his brother's apartment reading the note of directions for his departure, an overwhelming love for Russian folk-life possessed him and in this mood he sat down at the piano and improvised the theme of the Chorus of Welcome to Tsar Ivan in *The Maid of Pskov*.

He had a wonderful time in the country—enjoying the folk-dancing, horseback riding, and exchange of musical ideas with Borodin whose song *The Sea Princess* was composed during this visit.

Greatly refreshed by this experience, Rimsky-Korsakov, upon his return to St. Petersburg, wrote the third movement of *Antar* and several numbers for *The Maid of Pskov*. Later in the season *Antar* and these fragments of his opera were given at a Russian Musical Society concert under Balakirev. Rimsky-Korsakov had been invited to conduct his own compositions but the Minister of Marine thought such a public appearance unfitting for a Royal Officer. The composer was permitted, however, to sit on the platform and acknowledge the applause!

At the beginning of 1869, carrying out the wishes of Alexander Dargomyzhsky who died in January of that year, Rimsky-Korsakov began the scoring of *The Stone Guest*. Meanwhile he progressed with his own *Maid of Pskov* and revised the orchestration of *Sadko*. Throughout his life—at each stage of his learning—back he would go to his earlier compositions to improve them.

During the fall of 1871, Voin Rimsky-Korsakov's health made it necessary for him to close his flat and leave the city. Nikolai decided to take a room with Mussorgsky. Then it was that the two composers took turns using the single table and piano—with Rimsky-Korsakov working on *The Maid of Pskov* and Mussorgsky adding to his *Boris Godunov*.

Meanwhile an astonishing thing had happened to Rimsky-Korsakov. Out of a clear sky had come an invitation to teach practical composition and instrumentation and to direct the orchestra class at the St. Petersburg Conservatory. Thus it was that though still in the Navy he became a full-fledged professor! And as he himself expressed it, "one of its best and possibly its very best *pupil.*"

That winter of 1872 brought many changes into Rimsky-Korsakov's life. His brother Voin had died in the previous November, depriving him of a "second" father; he had taken on this amazing role of the professor; and then he became engaged to Nadejda Purgold. Being both a fine musician and an intelligent woman, she contributed greatly, thereafter, to the course of his life. It was she, in fact, who on their betrothal day had introduced him to some of Gogol's stories and had insisted that he write an opera on *May Night.*

Rimsky-Korsakov was fast becoming a professional musician in matter of fact if not in training. Dargomyzhsky's *The Stone Guest* with his orchestration attracted favorable attention at its first performance in February, 1872, and then came complicated plans for his own opera, *The Maid of Pskov.* According to an edict of Nicolas I, in 1837, no member of the Romanov family might be depicted on the stage in an opera. And since Ivan the Terrible—a Romanov—was one of the chief characters in *The Maid of Pskov*, its production seemed doomed. But Rimsky-Korsakov was not easily discouraged. Remembering that Krabbe, the Minister of Marine, had been particularly kind to him since the death of his brother Voin, Rimsky-Korsakov decided to appeal to him. And lo, the permission was granted!

Then in the summer of that year 1872 Rimsky-Korsakov and Nadejda

Purgold were married. Modest Mussorgsky acted as best man and wished them God-speed as they went off for a holiday to the south. After a happy summer spent in Switzerland and Italy they returned by way of Vienna and Warsaw, eager to establish their home in St. Petersburg and to begin rehearsals on *The Maid of Pskov.*

After the usual complications with manager and singers, the rehearsals began; and the opening performance, in January 1873, at the Marinsky Theater met with real success.

Topping this event came a complete change in Rimsky-Korsakov's official position. In a great burst of enthusiasm, Krabbe, the Minister of Marine, created for him a new post—that of Inspector of Bands—at a fine salary. Thus it was that in May of that year, Rimsky-Korsakov, relieved of the double role—professor-officer—became collegiate assessor as a private citizen.

And to everyone's amazement—particularly the long-established band-masters—he took his new duties seriously. Something theatrical in his nature responded to the salutes-of-attention, accorded him on his inspection tours; and he became a bit of the tyrant in the eyes of these Naval Bands. Small matter that he knew little about band instruments. He would learn!

Accordingly, when he and Nadejda went off to Pargolvo that summer their luggage took on the appearance of a small band. A flute, horn, clarinet, trombone and several other instruments kept them company. And with the aid of various charts and diagrams—despite the agony of their neighbors—Rimsky-Korsakov learned how each was played. Not content with *learning* the way they played, he set about the colossal task of writing a treatise with intricate diagrams on each instrument. Of course, *he* learned as he wrote. And although the venture was abandoned after two years' work, his own orchestration benefited enormously.

During the same summer he put himself through a rigid course in musical theory for, though a conservatory professor, Rimsky-Korsakov knew that there was much to learn. Then with the help of Tchaikovsky's "Harmony" and counterpoint texts by Cherubini and Bellermann, he began—what he called—his third symphony as a practical example of his *new* knowledge.

39

Back home in St. Petersburg at the end of August, the Rimsky-Korsakov's first child was born and he was named Michail or "Misha."

And still another new experience came to Rimsky-Korsakov that season in his first appearance as a conductor. The success of this occasion resulted in his being asked to take the place of Balakirev—who had practically retired from the musical world—as director of the Free School of Music. Rimsky-Korsakov accepted the invitation but did not become active in the work until the following autumn.

Meanwhile that summer, Rimsky-Korsakov with his wife and young son, went to a naval base on the Black Sea where Rimsky-Korsakov took charge of certain changes in the Naval Band. While there, they took a trip into the southern Crimea. Rimsky-Korsakov was fascinated by what he called gypsy music played in the streets from morning until night; and he returned to St. Petersburg with this oriental music ringing in his ears.

But for the moment he had no time for such flights of fancy. He must keep his nose to the grindstone. He must learn, learn, learn, until—as he put it—technique had entered his flesh and blood. Busy with a massed naval band concert, the reorganization of the Free School and his increasing interest in the early composers—due to his studies in fugue and counterpoint— Rimsky-Korsakov was a stranger that year to many of his former friends. Mussorgsky, whose very life-blood depended upon spontaneous musical expression, had no patience with this new phase in Rimsky-Korsakov. In fact, everyone except Borodin and Tchaikovsky—who admired such industry— made great fun of his endless writing of fugues.

He rewrote *Antar;* and he rewrote *The Maid of Pskov* until nobody was pleased with it—including himself! Then just when a worried observer might have thought that he was buried beneath his studies forever and forever he became genuinely interested in folk-songs, through Balakirev's awakening in that direction; and he brought forth his own *Collection of One Hundred Russian Folk-Songs.* At about the same time—again at Balakirev's invitation —he helped edit a special edition of Glinka's operas. Once again Rimsky-Korsakov was moved—as he had been in his early youth—by the simple, natural beauty of Glinka's music.

40

These two interruptions to his ever-lasting technical studies contributed to his beginning work—in February 1878—on the opera *May Night*. Nadejda was delighted and the score grew with such spontaneous inspiration that in April a great portion of it was played for a gathering of Mussorgsky, Cui, Stassov, and Rimsky-Korsakov's pupil, Anatol Liadov, to their warm and hearty approval.

Then as a welcome change from serious matters, Rimsky-Korsakov joined Borodin, Cui and Liadov in the writing of the famous *Paraphrases*, based on a polka theme of Borodin's. What fun they had! Rimsky-Korsakov, industrious as usual, wrote more than could be included in the collection when it was printed; and he was particularly pleased with his fugue on B-A-C-H, written to the accompaniment to the polka theme. Mussorgsky had been asked to contribute but it was not in his nature to conform to a pattern, even in fun, and after one unsuccessful attempt he refused to bother his head with the affair. Franz Liszt, on the contrary, was so pleased when he saw the *Paraphrases* that he added a version of his own and sent it with a letter of congratulation to the Russian pranksters.

Rimsky-Korsakov spent the summer of 1878 working on *May Night* in the country at Ligovo where a second son, Andrei, was born. When the family returned to St. Petersburg in the fall the full score of *May Night*, with the exception of the Overture was finished and it was at once accepted for production to be given during the season of 1879-80.

Meanwhile Rimsky-Korsakov conducted four important Free Music Concerts that included three choruses from *May Night*, the Pimen's cell scene from Mussorgsky's *Boris Godunov*, and several selections from Borodin's *Prince Igor*. Poor Borodin! He was such a busy, generous man that getting out his own work was a real problem. And what a time Rimsky-Korsakov had —prodding him along so that the *Prince Igor* excerpts would be ready, as announced, for the concert. Finally, at the last minute, Anatol Liadov and Rimsky-Korsakov took upon themselves the scoring of the Polovtsian Dances from *Igor*. As the parts were hastily written in pencil, Borodin covered the sheets of paper with liquid gelatine to keep them from smudging and then hung them on the line to dry!

41

The Rimsky-Korsakovs again spent the summer at Ligovo where Rimsky-Korsakov wrote a quartet based on Russian folk-tunes, and started a fantastic orchestral piece on Pushkin's Prologue to *Russlan and Ludmilla*.

Returning to St. Petersburg, he began the revision of his early *Overture on Three Russian Themes*. At the same time he was busy orchestrating the Persian Dances from Mussorgsky's opera, *Khovanschina*, for one of the Free School Concerts. Then came rehearsal for *May Night*, followed by its first performance at the beginning of the year 1880. Among the singers was the father of Igor Stravinsky, composer of *Petroushka* and *The Firebird*.

Then in February Rimsky-Korsakov began work on an opera based on A. N. Ostrovsky's play, *The Snow Maiden*. He had previously read this Russian fairy tale without being moved, but suddenly he was awakened to its natural charm and beauty. Why! it was the very subject for a lovely fairy opera! And he began at once to jot down in a great book of music-paper whole sections of the music. Filled with these plans, he took advantage of a trip to Moscow—where he went to conduct a concert—to visit Ostrovsky and obtain permission to use his play. The author, pleased with Rimsky-Korsakov's ideas, gave his consent and presented the composer with a copy of the play.

Summer that year brought a new vacation residence for the Rimsky-Korsakov family. And it proved to be an ideal setting for *The Snow Maiden*. It was an old house on a large estate, situated some twenty miles beyond Looga. Rimsky-Korsakov was delighted—"it was the first time in my life I had the opportunity of spending the summer in a genuine Russian countryside. A picturesque location, charming groves, a large forest, fields of rye, buckwheat, flax, wheat, many scattered villages, a river, a lake for bathing, a large lake for scenery." And even the old Russian names of the villages fascinated him—Kanyezerye, Podberyezye, Kopytyets, Dremyach, and Khvostmya.

The Snow Maiden music grew in leaps and bounds in these surroundings. Much of it was tried out on an old piano, tuned a tone too low, that Rimsky-Korsakov called "the piano in B-flat." He began—as he had done in *May Night*—by writing out the full score but his musical ideas jumping ahead of his fingers, forced him to change to jotting down a rough sketch for voices and piano. And on top of this, he found time to take long walks with Nadejda, help her pick mushrooms and assist with jelly making.

He returned to St. Petersburg in September with not only the lovely *Snow Maiden* finished in its piano-vocal score, but a complete orchestral piece, *Legend,* and some of the orchestration of his *Russian Quartet.*

In addition to his official duties Rimsky-Korsakov started at once on the orchestration of *The Snow Maiden* and when the six-hundred-page score was finished in the spring he felt within himself that he had become a mature musician. And being a realist, he was not modest in affirming that though Balakirev, Borodin, Cui and Mussorgsky had greater talent than he, they lacked his technical skill, and he did not envy them one bit!

Meanwhile Mussorgsky having taken ill shortly after one of the Free Music Concerts, died that spring, leaving the editing of all his works to Rimsky-Korsakov. This immense task, taking a good two years' work, Rimsky-Korsakov set about doing with methodical labor. Music scholars since that time who have discovered Mussorgsky's music in its original form have resented Rimsky-Korsakov's pedantic handling of the scores, but in all fairness to Rimsky-Korsakov he did at least make available—workman-like editions of Mussorgsky's music for practical production.

The next season Rimsky-Korsakov resigned as director of the Free School —this position being resumed by Balakirev—and devoted himself to the orchestration of Mussorgsky's *Khovanschina* and the rehearsal of his own *Snow Maiden.* Its first performance took place at the beginning of the year 1882 at about the same time as the birth of another son, Volodia. The opera was fairly well received but, for some reason, it was not given its just credit by the press.

Khovanschina occupied him during that summer except for a trip made to Moscow to conduct two concerts for the All-Russian Art and Industrial Exhibition. He included on one of the programs the First Symphony by one of his most brilliant pupils—Sasha Glasunov. Now it so happened that Mitrofan Petrovitch Belaiev, a wealthy music lover, having heard this symphony previously at a Free School Concert, came to Moscow specially to hear it again. Introducing himself to Rimsky-Korsakov at the first rehearsal, he asked permission to attend all the rehearsals, and this meeting of Rimsky-Korsakov and Belaiev proved an important link in the chain of Russian musical history.

The year 1883 brought a new official appointment to Rimsky-Korsakov. At the Accession of Alexander III to the throne after the assassination of Alexander II, changes were made in the Imperial Chapel, and it fell to Bala-kirev's lot to act as Musical Director with Rimsky-Korsakov as his assistant. Rimsky-Korsakov, at first, found his new duties interesting, and, with his increasing family, he welcomed the additional income, but within a year he was bored almost to distraction with the task and irked because he was writing no music.

Meanwhile Krabbe having been replaced by a new Minister of Marine, Rimsky-Korsakov lost his position as Inspector of Bands—that office having been abolished for the sake of economy. And gradually his life took on an entirely different pattern. Of the original group, only Borodin and Stassov continued to visit the Rimsky-Korsakovs. Now the new generation—most of them former pupils of Rimsky-Korsakov made up the Circle—Liadov, Glasunov, Arensky—all of them trained musicians. How different from the groping young amateurs who made up the "Mighty Handful!"

Belaiev became the new pivot about which the group gravitated. They met at his house every Friday night to play string quartets after which supper was served. Then back they would go to their music-making—with Glasunov, usually, playing some new composition. And still at three or so in the morning when the party broke up Belaiev would often carry off the more wide-awake ones to a restaurant for an early breakfast.

Through the accident of having paid for a private edition of Glasunov's First Symphony, Belaiev found himself a music publisher. Likewise, through the experience of hiring an auditorium and the Opera Orchestra for a performance of some of Glasunov's works, he eventually started a series of concerts known as the "Russian Symphony Concerts." In both of these ventures, Rimsky-Korsakov became his right-hand man, and the new publishing firm naturally published many of his compositions.

Meanwhile Rimsky-Korsakov had fallen into a period of creative inactivity. He did little except brush up some of his early works, and write a text-book on harmony for his Chapel pupils. In the fall of 1885 he collaborated with Borodin, Liadov and Glasunov on a quartet to celebrate Belaiev's name-day, and he wrote the *Fantasia on Russian Themes* for Krasnokutsky, the violin teacher of the Imperial Chapel.

Then in February 1887, Borodin died leaving another "duty" to be performed by the willing Rimsky-Korsakov. He and Glasunov set to work at once to finish and orchestrate Borodin's *Prince Igor*. That summer the Rimsky-Korsakovs took a house at Nikolskoe on a lovely lake, and like magic, the old creative urge returned. In addition to *Prince Igor*, he resumed work on what was intended to be a companion piece to his *Fantasia on Russian Themes*, but what developed into the famous orchestral work, *Spanish Capriccio* or *Spanish Caprice*. Rimsky-Korsakov was delighted with the sparkling result, emphasizing the fact that it was not a mere feat in orchestration, but that the orchestration was the "very essence of the composition." It was given its first performance at the fifth Russian Symphony Concert of the season in December, 1887, with Rimsky-Korsakov as conductor. The audience was as delighted as the orchestra had been at rehearsals, and the deafening rounds of applause continued until the piece was repeated on the spot!

Sketches for two other orchestral pieces of similar brilliance followed immediately—the *Easter Overture* and *Schéhérazade*. They were both finished that summer in the country at Nejgovitsky. These three orchestral pieces rounded out a period of brilliant orchestration; then Rimsky-Korsakov looked for new worlds to conquer.

And the "new world" appeared that very next season when Angelo Neumann brought Wagner's complete *Ring* cycle to St. Petersburg. Rimsky-Korsakov and Glasunov practically lived at the Marinsky Theater during rehearsals —following the scores note by note. What an experience—even for a composer of as brilliant accomplishments as Rimsky-Korsakov! He was acquainted with *Lohengrin* and some of Wagner's other works, but this introduction to the mature "Wagner" completely astounded him. Both he and

Glasunov were amazed at Wagner's handling of instruments and Rimsky-Korsakov admitted, "thenceforth Wagner's methods gradually permeated our orchestral writing."

The conducting of six Russian Symphony Concerts that season left little time for composition, but in February a new work got under way through an accidental suggestion. A group of friends—Stassov, Liadov, Glasunov, Belaiev and the Rimsky-Korsakovs met at Borodin's old home on the second anniversary of his death to play some of his music. While they were playing over and discussing the possibility of orchestrating Borodin's fourth act of *Mlada*, Liadov exclaimed, "Nikolai, what a subject for you!"

"So it is!" responded Rimsky-Korsakov.

And he immediately set to work on his own libretto of it—"just like Wagner."

But work on it was interrupted during the summer by a trip to Paris for the World Exhibition. Belaiev financed two all-Russian concerts for this occasion and Rimsky-Korsakov was the conductor. Leaving the children with his mother, he and Nadejda prepared for a real holiday. But as soon as the concerts—artistically successful but not well attended for lack of advertising—were over, the Rimsky-Korsakovs hurried home by way of Switzerland and Vienna. And by the end of the summer the first draft of *Mlada* was finished.

Many events interfered with the orchestrating of this new opera. In April, 1890, he went to Brussels to conduct a concert of Russian music. Back home he found Nadejda seriously ill with diphtheria. Their son Andrei then contracted the disease; later in the season Rimsky-Korsakov's aged mother died; in the same year the Rimsky-Korsakovs lost their youngest child and soon afterward two-year-old Masha fell dangerously ill.

Little wonder that Rimsky-Korsakov did scarcely any creative work in this period. He tried his hand at a new version of *The Maid of Pskov;* re-orchestrated *Sadko;* thought about doing an opera on the "Sadko" subject, and started to write a book. But this proved to be a crucial point in his life when nothing seemed worth the effort and dull pains in his head made composing irksome.

Mlada, having been completed under trying circumstances, was given in the fall of 1892 without helping the composer's spirits one whit.

Thoroughly alarmed at her husband's ill health, Nadejda insisted that he consult a physician. "Rest, complete rest from music and reading," was the verdict. "Rest—and lots of outdoor exercise."

But rest and long walks did little good. And in the fall Rimsky-Korsakov turned over the conducting of the Russian Symphony Concerts to Liadov and Glasunov. At the same time he made an attempt, unsuccessfully, to resign from his Chapel post. Then relentlessly, fate continued her spell of ill-fortune, for little Masha grew worse instead of better, prompting Nadejda to take her, in the spring of 1893, to the Crimea where they hoped that the southern climate would be beneficial. Rimsky-Korsakov joined them there in May as soon as his official duties were over and tried his utmost to finish the new orchestration of *The Maid of Pskov,* while at the same time he was writing his memoirs—hoping to leave a faithful record of an important period in Russian musical history.

Returning to St. Petersburg in the early fall to resume his Chapel duties, he was followed by a telegram announcing Masha's death. But whereas this family loss increased his inactivity, the death of Peter Ilyitch Tchaikovsky in October of that year, served to awaken him.

"Why! the first Russian Symphony Concert of the season must be dedicated to Tchaikovsky. And of course I must conduct it."

And before he realized what was happening he had resumed the conducting of the series. Then during an excursion to Odessa to conduct another Tchaikovsky memorial concert, Rimsky-Korsakov became re-inspired to write an opera based on Gogol's *Christmas Eve.* Tchaikovsky having used the same story in his opera, *Vakula the Smith,* had kept Rimsky-Korsakov—though long attracted by the subject—from using it before. Now he could write his version without giving the impression that he was rivalling Tchaikovsky.

Finding a new country house at Vetchasha in the Luga district that summer of 1894, Rimsky-Korsakov settled down to work with renewed strength. And while working on his *Christmas Eve* another idea—long brewing—burst forth full-blown—an opera based on *Sadko*. By sheer effort he thrust this aside until *Christmas Eve* was finished.

He returned to St. Petersburg in September with a complete sketch and one hundred fully orchestrated pages of *Christmas Eve*. Finishing the orchestration that winter, he freely admitted to someone that he evidently preferred orchestrating to composing. Then having won a special dispensation from the Court in regard to portraying an Empress on the stage, Rimsky-Korsakov went back to Vetchasha the summer of 1895—eager to work on *Sadko*—with production plans for *Christmas Eve* entirely set.

Back home in September with a good bit of *Sadko* finished, he immediately concerned himself with *Christmas Eve* rehearsals. But it proved an ill-fated production. Members of the Imperial family, attending the final dress rehearsal, were horrified at the sight of the "Empress Catherine" on the stage, and much to Rimsky-Korsakov's disgust this soprano role had to be changed to that of a baritone before the Tsar would give his consent to the production. Rimsky-Korsakov, was in fact, so mortified that he refused to attend the opening performance, given at the end of the year 1895, at the Marinsky Theater.

The Rimsky-Korsakovs went that summer to Schmerdovitsy where Rimsky-Korsakov finished *Sadko* and began another book on orchestration. He was delighted with *Sadko* and its successful completion tapped a new fountain of inspiration that brought forth forty melodic songs, an opera—*Mozart and Salieri*—a cantata, a trio, and a string quartet. And just to top these off Rimsky-Korsakov found time for work on his important orchestration book.

Then in the fall of 1897, due to the complications in the acceptance of *Sadko* by the St. Petersburg Theater Directorate, Rimsky-Korsakov promptly withdrew the offer of it, and handed it over to the Momontov Company in Moscow where it was produced at the Solodovikovsky Theater. Shortly after the new year this Moscow company visited St. Petersburg and opened its season with a brilliant performance of *Sadko*, conducted by Rimsky-Korsakov himself.

Thus he continued with tremendous energy—finishing the revised version of *The Maid of Pskov*, writing a one-act opera, as well as a full length one—

48

The Tsar's Bride. This was produced in October of 1899 in Moscow by Momontov who in the meantime had given the revised *Maid of Pskov* with the famous bass singer, Feodor Chaliapin, then a young man, in the role of Ivan the Terrible by which name the opera is now generally known.

Then followed the delightful opera, *Tsar Saltan,* based on a Pushkin fairy tale. That finished, Rimsky-Korsakov decided to write something non-Russian and accordingly, he chose the melodrama, *Servilia,* laid in ancient Rome. Following a trip to Brussels, he set to work on it at once; continued it during a stay at Strasbourg in Germany where his son Andrei was attending the University and finished the rough draft of it while spending the summer with his family in Switzerland.

That December of 1900 marked the thirty-fifth anniversary of Rimsky-Korsakov's first public appearance as a composer, and various musical societies—both in Moscow and St. Petersburg—celebrated the occasion. As a matter of fact, he was feted so well and so long that the situation became irksome. Having accepted one invitation, he could not in fairness refuse another, and on it went until he declared, "I wish no one such a jubilee!"

Soon he was busy with a new opera, *Kashchei,* on which his daughter Sonia helped with the score. That finished, he immediately turned to another called *Pan Voevoda,* which he finished—together with a new scoring of Dargomyzhsky's *Stone Guest*—while at Heidelberg where Andrei was then studying and where Nikolai Rimsky-Korsakov, the master and Igor Stravinsky, the pupil, met for the first time.

Before *Pan Voevoda* was entirely scored, Rimsky-Korsakov was at work on still another opera—*Kitej.* And then in December of that year 1903, Belaiev died, leaving his publishing house, the Russian Symphony Concerts, and his various musical prizes in the hands of Rimsky-Korsakov, Glasunov and Liadov. Straight-off Rimsky-Korsakov wrote an orchestral piece in Belaiev's memory, *At the Grave,* which he conducted at the season's first Russian Symphony Concert.

The following summer was marked by deep concern over the Russian disasters in the Japanese War and strangely enough, Rimsky-Korsakov was to suffer indirectly himself. By fall, St. Petersburg was clothed in a spirit

49

of revolution to which the Conservatory Students contributed their share. It so happened that when Bernhard, the director, used tactless methods in handling the situation, Rimsky-Korsakov stood up for the students' rights, and thereby won the reputation of being a ringleader of student revolution. The whole affair finally resulted in both Rimsky-Korsakov and Bernhard being dismissed and the Conservatory temporarily closed.

This move directed against a man of Rimsky-Korsakov's reputation, brought a storm of protests. The papers were glowing in his praise; and a concert was given in his honor at which the police had to be called to stop a demonstration. Fearing further trouble, the St. Petersburg police banned the next Russian Symphony Concert and, in fact, forbade the performance of any of Rimsky-Kohsakov's music!

This naturally increased his popularity but at the same time contributed to his seeking rest and peace. Withdrawing to Vetchasha, he busied himself with his autobiography, *My Musical Life*, and his book on orchestration.

Finding the Conservatory closed upon his return to St. Petersburg that fall, Rimsky-Korsakov accepted some private pupils at his home. Eventually the Conservatory reopened and he was reinstated, but soon trouble broke out again and at one stormy meeting Rimsky-Korsakov marched out of the room, declaring that he washed his hands of the Conservatory. Although he was brought back after some persuasion, he returned with little enthusiasm.

That summer the Rimsky-Korsakovs spent their holiday at Riva on Lake Garda where Rimsky-Korsakov finished the record of his life and made up his mind to compose no more.

Within six weeks after his return to St. Petersburg the jaunty *Coq d'or* or *Golden Cockerel* was under way!

While he was happily at work on this droll opera—coincident with the celebration of the twenty-fifth anniversary of his worthy pupil, Glasunov—a brilliant new star joined his family of private pupils—Igor Stravinsky.

In February of that year 1907, *Kitej* was given at the Marinsky Theater in St. Petersburg with tremendous success, after which Rimsky-Korsakov wanted to settle down to his *Golden Cockerel*. But a new force that had come into Russian art life persuaded him, against his will, to go to Paris for a spring festival of five Russian concerts. This typhoon of energy was Sergei Diaghilev, one of the greatest impresarios, or managers, of all time—the one whose name will be forever linked with the Russian Ballet.

Accordingly, in May, Rimsky-Korsakov and several members of his family journeyed to Paris where music from *Tsar Saltan*, *Christmas Eve*, *Mlada*, *Sadko* and *Snow Maiden* were played on the Diaghilev programs, some of which the composer conducted. During this enforced Paris visit, Rimsky-Korsakov heard some of the *new* music of the day—including Alexander Scriabin's *Poem of Ecstasy*, and Richard Strauss's *Salome*. He also met these two composers, as well as Claude Debussy. And the story goes that upon hearing Debussy's opera, *Pelleas and Melisande*, Rimsky-Korsakov declared, "I will have nothing more to do with this music, for fear I shall develop a liking for it!"

As a matter of fact, he could scarcely wait to get back to his *Golden Cockerel*. After returning to St. Petersburg, they went immediately to the beautiful Liubensk estate, near Vetchasha where the full score of two acts were finished and the third act sketched by the end of August.

On his return to St. Petersburg Rimsky-Korsakov was pestered with all sorts of honors from the outside world, while Diaghilev was dickering for a *Sadko* production at the Grand Opera in Paris, and *The Snow Maiden* was being prepared for an Opera-Comique production under N. N. Tcherepnin.

At home, political complications delayed the acceptance of the *Golden Cockerel* for production, though the score was being published.

Then in the midst of correcting the Golden Cockerel proofs, Rimsky-Korsakov was stricken with a severe heart attack.

"Complete rest," ordered the doctor.

But Rimsky-Korsakov did not know the meaning of the word. Consequently, after a few days, another attack followed. This time his family and friends managed to keep him in bed for a week, but for not another minute! Back he went—with the help of Maximilian Steinberg—to the Cockerel proofs and his orchestration book.

In June his daughter, Nadia, was married in the village church to Maximilian Steinberg, but Rimsky-Korsakov was not well enough to attend. The

51

following day he had a bad heart attack. And on Sunday, June 21, 1908, after having written a few pages in his orchestration book the day before, Nikolai Rimsky-Korsakov died.

His strange world—half fancy and half reality—goes on in his music. Although he was not one of the musical giants—such as Beethoven, Bach, or Wagner—he, nevertheless, carved a lightning-path of color in sound—exemplified in Schéhérazade—that cannot possibly be mistaken for anyone other than Rimsky-Korsakov!

HUMPERDINCK

ENGELBERT HUMPERDINCK

Creator of "Haensel and Gretel"

BORN 1854—DIED 1921

Engelbert humperdinck—whose very name sounds like that of a character in a fairy tale—was born on the first day of September, 1854, at Siegburg, near Bonn, Germany—the birthplace of Ludwig van Beethoven. Rimsky-Korsakov was a boy of ten and John Philip Sousa—who was destined to become "The March King" of America—was born the same year.

As a small child he loved the songs his mother sang to him and his sister Adelheide to put them to sleep. And while he was still quite young, little tunes of his own went buzzing about in his head. But when the time came for Engelbert to prepare himself for a life-work, his parents persuaded him to study architecture. Music was wonderful to enjoy as a recreation, but as a career—architecture was much more practical. Little did they know that their son's name would go down in history—not as a builder of sensible, put-your-finger-on-things like bank buildings and churches, but—as the architect of a ginger bread house!

Being a dutiful son, his studies at the Paderborn High School all pointed in the direction of architecture. When he went on to Cologne, architecture was still the goal of his studies. But fate stepped into the picture, when Engelbert was asked to compose some incidental music to Goethe's *Claudia von Willabella*. How he enjoyed it! *This* was what he wanted to do for the rest of his life.

Accordingly, he took his courage in hand and went to the distinguished composer and teacher, Ferdinand Hiller, with the music he had just written. Hiller was sufficiently impressed with this youthful effort to encourage its creator to devote himself to music.

And thus it was that Humperdinck entered the Cologne Conservatory that fall as a student of music. He studied harmony and composition with Hiller and Friedrich Gernsheim; counterpoint with Gustav Jensen; piano with Isador Seiss and Eduard Mertke; and violoncello with Jacques Rensburg and a man by the name of Ehlert. At the end of four years, having won the Mozart scholarship at Frankfort, he went to Munich where he studied two years at the Munich Conservatory under Franz Lachner, Josef Rheinberger, and Karl Barmann.

Then upon winning the Berlin Mendelssohn Prize in 1879, Humperdinck went to Italy for a couple of years. And there fate again played an important part in his career. It so happened that Richard Wagner, having greatly overworked during the composition of his last music drama, *Parsifal*, had gone, in January 1880, with his family to Naples where they settled down for the winter at the Villa d'Angri. When Humperdinck, who was in Rome, heard that his great idol, Richard Wagner, was so close at hand, nothing could keep him away from Naples.

Arriving at the Villa d'Angri at the beginning of March, he sent in his card on which was flamboyantly inscribed: "Companion of the Order of the Grail"—this being an organization of young Munich musicians who were ardent crusaders for Wagner and his festival theater at Bayreuth. The servant to whom Humperdinck handed the card, having been cautioned by Wagner's loyal wife, Cosima, to admit no one, glanced at the card and said, "The Master is not at home."

But just as the crestfallen young composer had reached the outer gate, he heard his name being called, "Herr Humperdinck, the Master will see you."

Wagner, meanwhile, having seen the card, was genuinely amused and could not resist meeting his knightly admirer. They liked each other at once, and soon Humperdinck had become a member of the Wagner inner circle.

Returning to Naples in May at Wagner's invitation, after a trip to Sicily, Humperdinck spent many an evening in the Wagner home—playing over

56

parts of *Parsifal* and discussing music to his heart's content. And Wagner, who had a great capacity for recognizing and encouraging talent, now adopted Humperdinck into his musical family and called him—"Humpschen."

Then "Humpschen" was invited to Bayreuth to help with the preparations for *Parsifal*. The Wagners returned there in November while Humperdinck followed at the beginning of the new year—eager to help the Master. Settling near Wahnfried, the Wagner home, Humperdinck made a connected copy of the Parsifal score as Wagner sent over the finished pages. This experience of watching the score grow page by page, together with the wonderful evenings spent at Wahnfried, proved of great value to the young composer.

Meanwhile he had won the Meyerbeer Prize of four thousand five hundred marks from the Berlin Academy of Arts with three compositions: an overture, a cantata, and an eight-part fugue for double choir. According to the conditions of the prize, he was supposed to go to France to study, but wishing to remain with Wagner as long as he was needed, Humperdinck obtained a postponement from the Academy.

Following the score-copying came actual work on the production itself, including the coaching of some of the singers. And then to Humperdinck's great delight, Wagner turned over the organization and training of the Grail Chorus to him.

But his great moment arrived in June 1882, when at some of the final rehearsals of *Parsifal*, it was found that the revolving set in the Transformation Scene moved too slowly for the amount of music Wagner had provided. After several attempts to adjust the machinery's movements to the music, Wagner, completely exhausted, declared, "I wash my hands of the whole affair."

Then it was that Humperdinck slipped quietly away, wrote a few bars of music to fill in the gap and took them, with fear in his heart to Wagner.

"That will do it!" said Wagner.

So it did; the next time the scene was rehearsed, music and machinery fit perfectly. And though later the scene-shifting was speeded up so that Wagner's music could be used in its original form, Humperdinck had enjoyed his moment!

As soon as the Bayreuth Festival of 1882 was over and *Parsifal* had been gloriously produced before an audience, made up of persons from all over the world, Humperdinck left for Paris to fulfill the conditions of the Meyerbeer Prize. But in December, Wagner—who was then in Venice—sent an urgent letter: "Come conduct my symphony for Cosima's birthday!"

Accordingly, off went Humperdinck to Venice to help prepare a surprise performance of Wagner's early symphony. Wagner in the end—though a very sick man—did the conducting himself, but Humperdinck was on hand to help.

After Wagner's death in February, Humperdinck continued throughout the years to be a member of the Wagner family; and it was he who had charge of the musical education of Siegfried, Wagner's only son.

For a time, Humperdinck traveled and studied. Then in 1885 he went to Spain where he taught in the Barcelona Conservatory for two years. Back in Germany, he taught for a time in Cologne; worked for Schott's, a famous music publishing firm at Mainz; and then in 1890 he became a professor of the Hoch Conservatory in Frankfort where he also served as music critic for the *Frankfurter Zeitung*.

Meanwhile he was composing music including two choral ballads, *The Luck of Edenhall*, and *The Pilgrim to Kevlaar*; but it was not until the year 1893 that Humperdinck came into his own in an extraordinary way. In the spring of 1891, Frau Adelheide Wette—who was Humperdinck's sister, now grown up and the mother of children of her own—wanted to put on a little fairy play for her family. "Engelbert, do write a little tune for these lines— 'Brother, come and dance with me....'"

And she was so delighted with what he wrote that she decided to write a little opera—with her brother—on the story of Haensel and Gretel for her children.

But once Humperdinck set his mind on the subject, the opera grew beyond the limits of a home theater. Adding his own personality, his own special ability to what he had learned from Wagner's scores, he created an opera, both unique and delightful. Whereas Wagner dealt with gods, giants, and lordly creatures, Humperdinck spun his music round fairy tale children—

58

using some of Wagner's methods including leading motives in the music to identify the characters and to tell the story,

Hermann Levi, who had conducted *Parsifal* at its first Bayreuth production, was delighted with *Haensel and Gretel* when it was brought to his attention, and contracted to do it at once at the Munich Opera. Meanwhile Richard Strauss wanted to give it at Weimar, the city consecrated to music by Franz Liszt. And it was at Weimar, on December 23, 1893, that the first performance of *Haensel and Gretel* took place, due to a necessary postponement of the Munich production.

This delightful fairy opera made no special impression on the theater management, but the public took it to its heart at once. Weimar loved it; Munich was equally pleased when it was given there; Berlin, Frankfort, Prague, Vienna, Dresden—all fell beneath *Haensel and Gretel's* spell.

This wonderful success made it possible for Humperdinck to retire to Boppard on the Rhine where he devoted most of his time to composing. He did, however, accept the directorship of the Master School Academy in Berlin, a post he held for twenty years.

Many compositions appeared through the years, including another opera, *Die Königskinder* (The King's Children), a comic opera called *The Unwilling Marriage*, and a great deal of incidental music, such as that to Shakespeare's plays: *The Tempest, Twelfth Night, The Winter's Tale, The Merchant of Venice; Maeterlinck's The Blue Bird;* and some to the famous Max Reinhardt production of *The Miracle.*

Honors came his way. He was made a Royal Professor; and he was appointed a member of the Royal Academy of Arts, eventually becoming its president. But when Humperdinck died on the 27th of September, 1921, at Neustraulitz, he was known as the composer of *Haensel and Gretel.* And *today* he is remembered as the composer of *Haensel and Gretel*—that delightful fairy opera—whose music is simple, yet subtly woven like the threads in a silken tapestry.

ELGAR

SIR EDWARD ELGAR

"For England and St. George!"

BORN 1857—DIED 1934

On JUNE 2, 1857, Edward William Elgar—England's first major composer since the days of Henry Purcell in the seventeenth century—was born at Broadheath, near Worcester, England. Johannes Brahms was twenty-four years old and Engelbert Humperdinck was a child of three.

It has been said that English cottages give the appearance of having risen from the soil on which they stand, and it was in a small village made up of such homes that young Elgar grew like-wise—from English *lad* to English *man*—Sir Edward Elgar!

His father, W. H. Elgar, who conducted a small music business in the city of Worcester, was also organist of the Roman Catholic Church of St. George. In addition, he played the violin, the viola, and piano; and was, indeed, one of the musical figures of Worcester. Edward's mother—whose name had been Anne Greening—brought to her home a knowledge and a love for literature. And little Edward, fascinated by the sound of the words, often begged her— long before he understood the meanings of the words—to read aloud or recite to him.

When Edward was about four years old, Mr. Elgar's increasing activities in Worcester prompted him to move his family there. And it was not long before his little son begged to be allowed to sit in the organ loft of St. George's while he practiced.

Then he must learn to play some instrument himself! Accordingly, he began—as most children do—with the piano, but for some reason this did not satisfy him. Turning to the violin, he found his true instrument. And though he did not become a great violinist, he learned to use the violin in a way that in later years gave the texture of his music a special quality.

His teacher was Frederick Spry who played the violin and led the orchestra of the Worcester Glee Club. Edward advanced rapidly on his chosen instrument and was soon playing in the orchestra along with his teacher. Eventually other members of the Elgar family joined the orchestra, resulting in something akin to English-Bach concerts.

When Edward was eleven years old he was sent to Littleton House, a small school in which twenty-five or thirty boys studied under a man whose name was Francis Reeve. This teacher proved very important in young Elgar's development. One day, during a discussion on the twelve apostles, Francis Reeve said to his pupils: "The apostles were poor men at the time of their calling; perhaps before the descent of the Holy Ghost not cleverer than some of you here."

This set young Elgar to thinking: resulting eventually in his oratorio, *The Apostles*. But long before that, the seeds of Mr. Reeve's statements bore fruit in other ways. Edward said to himself: "If the apostles—no cleverer than I— were thus inspired, why cannot I, if I work hard and have *faith*, also achieve spiritual help?"

Accordingly, he set to work to learn, learn, learn! He listened to music in St. George's Church where his father played the organ; he attended the services in Worcester Cathedral; he studied the Bible and the musical ritual of the Church; he experimented with various instruments in his father's shop, and began to compose pieces of his own with the help of books, for instance—Stainer's *Harmony*.

But the Elgar family was large, and the time had come when Edward must think about making a living. Accordingly, at sixteen—the year in which another important English composer, Ralph Vaughan Williams, was born— Edward Elgar was apprenticed to a Worcester solicitor. He was, at first, fascinated by this new life. Legal terms tripped off his tongue with the ease of a seasoned lawyer and Mr. Allan, the solicitor, told Edward's father that his son was a "bright lad." But the novelty wore off and the future composer asked himself, "What have weighty law problems to do with my oratorio on the apostles?"

The music inside him answered the question and he left Mr. Allan's law office in 1873—not without profit—for he had learned to weigh and consider a problem. Setting this knowledge immediately to work, he mapped out a way to make a living as a musician. He would establish himself in his own community as a violinist—both teacher and performer.

In addition to carrying out this plan, he helped in the Elgar music shop; became assistant organist to his father at St. George's Church; and mastered the technique of the bassoon in order to take part in wind-instrument performances with his brother who played the oboe. Soon he had become accompanist in the Worcester Glee Club; then violinist in the orchestra of the Worcester Festival Choral Society; he also wrote and arranged music right and left for the Worcester Glee Club. And the wonder is—that any time remained to teach the violin.

He was, however, successful enough in his violin activities to justify his going to London, in the summer of 1877, to take some violin lessons from Adolphe Pollitzer. At the first lesson, Pollitzer laid out a course of study for his new Worcester pupil and directed him to buy a certain book of exercises. At their second meeting, he asked Elgar, "Which exercise have you prepared?"

"All of them," answered Elgar.

Such was Elgar's capacity for work, and consequently though he had only money enough for a few lessons, he returned to Worcester vastly enriched by this short encounter with Adolphe Pollitzer.

Back home, he set himself the task of writing out a symphony in the exact framework of Mozart's G minor Symphony. And thirty years later he made the statement that he remembered no discipline from which he had learned so much. Then more and more music developed naturally from his various activities: as for instance, his *Introduction Overture*, which appeared, in 1878, on a Christy Minstrel concert program. Music had become his career and entirely through his own efforts!

In the year 1879 he was appointed conductor of the Worcester Glee Club and of the County Lunatic Asylum Band. This latter appointment—though strange-sounding—offered one more important step in Elgar's musical development. Spending one day of each week at the Asylum, it was his duty not only to train and conduct a band from among the attendants, but to train them individually on such varied instruments as the flute, oboe, clarinet; double bass, piano and violin. And on top of that, he composed and arranged special music for the Band, including a work with a typically Elgarian title—*Quadrille for an Eccentric Orchestra.*

The following year brought a visit to Paris where Elgar had a wonderful time—hearing new music; meeting new people; enjoying the novelty of going to the theater; and listening to Camille Saint-Saens play the organ at the famous Madeleine.

Each successive year in Elgar's life piled high—one on the other—new musical activities: in 1881 he began playing first violin in the Worcester Festival Orchestra; the following year he became first violinist in an important Birmingham orchestra. Then the Worcester Amateur Instrumental Society made him its conductor and program annotator, or editor: all this in addition to his teaching, organ-playing at St. George's and his music-writing.

Some of the music composed in the early years found a place later in his published works, including that which he wrote for a play, titled *The Wand of Youth*—a jolly family affair. In that instance, Elgar was not only called upon to use ingenuity in arranging music for the available players, but feeling the need of a double bass for his effects, he, with the help of his brother, broke up a packing case in his father's music shop and *made* a double bass!

By this time Elgar had given up any idea of becoming a concert violinist. He was going to be a composer and a *good* one. And since Germany was then the center of things musical—particularly Leipzig—it was to Leipzig that his thoughts continually turned. Finally, he had to give up any idea of studying there, but by carefully saving his money, he was able to visit Leipzig at the end of 1882. That visit helped to stimulate and crystallize his future.

Back home, he applied renewed energy to composing, and it was in the year 1883 that his first real encouragement came in this direction. His orchestral piece *Intermezzo: Sérénade mauresque* was successfully performed by Stockley's Birmingham Orchestra. The next year he wrote *Sevillana* expressly for the Worcester Philharmonic Society. And soon after its first performance, having been asked by Pollitzer—from whom he still took occasional lessons—whether he composed, he showed him *Sevillana*. Pollitzer introduced the young composer to August Manns, conductor of the Crystal Palace concerts in London, and this meeting resulted in the performance of *Sevillana* at the Crystal Palace the following July.

Elgar now took himself firmly in hand and went off to Scotland for a solitary pilgrimage into his own soul. He had accomplished certain things; there was a great deal to be done, and there was just so much energy. He came to the conclusion that traveling from pillar to post as a soloist was not his forte, and that for the sake of his composing he could not afford to spend one whole day at the Lunatic Asylum. His life belonged in the English countryside and his music would come out of it, providing he left himself sufficient freedom to create.

Then in September while playing in the Three Choirs Festival at Worcester, he came in contact with still another force of influence—Antonin Dvořák. The Bohemian composer, who had come to England to conduct his *Stabat Mater* and Second Symphony, stimulated Elgar tremendously and inspired him to go ahead, to be himself, to create!

Elgar did not, however, become famous overnight. Despite his many musical activities and the two or three successful performances of his music, the English people—outside Worcester—paid slight attention to their native son. Meanwhile having become organist of St. George's at his father's resignation of the post in 1885, and stimulated by the hearing of Dvořák's *Stabat Mater*, he began to compose a great deal of church music. He also continued to conduct various orchestras and to teach.

Then in October of 1886 a new pupil who was to have a guiding influence in his life came to him for lessons. Her name was Caroline Alice Roberts and on the eighth of May, 1889, she became Mrs. Edward Elgar. Just when doubts—not of his own ability—but of the possibilities of being heard were tormenting him, his wife entered the scene to strengthen, sustain and direct his path.

Soon after their marriage he gave up most of his Worcester appointments —with the exception of the Worcester Philharmonic Society and some of his pupils—and went with his wife to live in London. He wanted to hear music and to make publishing connections. Though he managed to get a few small things published, on the whole, the venture was not a successful one; and within a short time the Elgars returned to their native community and settled down at Malvern.

Thus life went on with a bit of encouragement here, a setback there, until finally in 1889 he was invited to write an orchestral piece for the Worcester Festival. Surely this would prove the golden wedge to recognition! It was the *Froissart* Overture that he wrote for the occasion—heading his score with a motto from Keats:

> "When chivalry
> Lifted up her lance on high."

Finished in the summer of 1890, the *Froissart* Overture revealed a mastery in the use of instruments which was to distinguish all of Elgar's mature work. Novello accepted it for publication in August; the Elgars' only child, a daughter named Carice—a combination of her mother's two names—was born the same month and the *Froissart* Overture was successfully performed under Elgar's direction at the Three Choirs Festival at Worcester in September. This was indeed a glorious year, but in spite of both spontaneous applause and critical praise, Elgar remained merely "the young Malvern composer."

Disappointed but undaunted, Elgar once again went back to his Malvern duties and kept doggedly at work. His next bit of encouragement came from Dr. Hugh Blair, organist of Worcester Cathedral. Coming upon Elgar in the midst of composing his first cantata, *The Black Knight*, Dr. Blair seeing the pages of manuscript lying about, asked, "What's this?"

Then picking up some of the sheets of paper, he began to play bits of the music on the piano. Suddenly turning to Elgar, he said, "If you will finish this I'll give it at the Worcester Festival Choral Society's concert next April."

The Black Knight—after its first performance—was given in various parts of England with increasing favor. Then in 1895 an arrangement for a small orchestra of *Salut d'Amour* won for him popular acclaim. This simple little piece, written originally for the piano, found itself arranged for practically every possible instrument and did much to make Elgar's name known.

Then two important choral works—the oratorio, *Lux Christi*, and the cantata, *King Olaf*, definitely established Elgar as an important composer. His works were now being given all over England; and when he had written the cantata, *The Banner of St. George*, and *The Imperial March* in honor of Queen Victoria's Diamond Jubilee, he was indeed England's famous composer!

Caractacus, a cantata in the grand manner followed, and then in 1899 he composed an orchestral work that has proved to be one of his most popular compositions—the *Enigma Variations*. Each section of the work is named after one of his friends—not the friend's *real* name—but one of Elgar's invention, such as "Nimrod" and "Dorabella." Hans Richter, the famous Wagnerian conductor, gave the *Enigma Variations* its first performance on June 19, 1899, at St. James Hall in London.

Elgar's fame was fast becoming a menace to his work; but at the beginning of 1900, turning his back, as far as possible, on the many festival and honorary activities offered him, he set to work on his famous oratorio, *The Dream of Gerontius*. This had been brewing in his mind for eleven years—since the day of his marriage to Caroline Alice Roberts, when they had received Cardinal Newman's famous poem, *The Dream of Gerontius*—as a wedding gift. This new work was given its first performance, under unfavorable circumstances, at the Birmingham Festival in October of 1900. It was not until the following year at Düsseldorf in Germany that it was recognized for its true worth. Later at another German performance, Richard Strauss drank a toast to this "progressive English musician"—and Elgar's name was well on its way to world renown.

Meanwhile he had written two of his famous marches—bearing the title

Pomp and Circumstance. And anyone who has ever heard a band play has heard Elgar's *Pomp and Circumstance* marches! His *Cockaigne* Overture belongs to this period; then came two delicate pieces for a small orchestra—*Dream Children*—based on Charles Lamb's essay—"We are nothing; less than nothing, and dreams. We are only what might have been."

Following this, he buried himself in the *Coronation Ode,* intended for performance at the coronation of King Edward VII. But due to the King's illness, the coronation was postponed and Elgar's *Coronation Ode* was not given until October 1902, when a great Thanksgiving concert was given at Queen's Hall in London to celebrate the King's recovery. Elgar conducted the *Odes* and the applause was so great at its conclusion that the manager of the concert was forced to ask the audience to permit the program to continue. Elgar had reached the hearts of the people and that is what he had always wanted to do.

Meanwhile he had taken a trip to Bayreuth where he heard Wagner's famous music drama *Parsifal.* This undoubtedly renewed his interest in the apostles—a subject which, as we know, had been brought to his attention by his schoolmaster. Deciding to write an oratorio on the theme, he buried himself in study and research: consulting scholars in both the Catholic and Anglican Church to supplement his own reading. The groundwork done, he wrote *The Apostles* during the first half of 1903, partly at his home, Craeg Lea, at Malvern, and partly at a place called Birchwood, far removed from every-day matters.

One welcome introduction came on the sixth of June when his *Dream of Gerontius* was given a glorious production at Westminster Cathedral in London. This time it was thoroughly appreciated: one critic being in abject admiration; another, calling it "a work of imperishable beauty."

Then on October 14th of that year, his oratorio, *The Apostles,* was given at the Birmingham Festival. This new work convinced most of the doubtful ones that Elgar was a creative artist. Just when many composers were certain that the oratorio form of music had been used up by such giant examples as Handel's *Messiah* and Mendelssohn's *Elijah,* here was Elgar with his own methods—bringing new life to this type of music!

The next important event came in the three-day Elgar Festival, held at Covent Garden on March 14, 1904. No other English composer had been given this honor, and at the concluding concert, after conducting his recently finished overture, *In the South,* he was accorded a genuine ovation.

Honors followed one after another: in April he was elected to the Athenaeum Club, indicating that he was a man of "distinguished eminence," and then in July he was Knighted. Henceforth he was Sir Edward Elgar— carrying out an unconscious prophecy of his youth, for the story goes that once when a schoolmaster asked him his name, he replied, "Edward Elgar." Whereupon, the teacher reminded him to say, "sir."

Back came the future composer-Knight's reply, "Sir Edward Elgar."

In spite of honors too numerous to mention, Elgar managed to continue his work and his next composition, *Introduction and Allegro* for strings, is regarded as unique in the world of string music. Given its first performance in March of 1905 in Queen's Hall, it embarked almost immediately on an American career. In June the Elgars went to America as guests of Professor S. S. Sanford of Yale University. And after being royally entertained and made Doctor of Music by Yale University, Elgar dedicated his lovely *Introduction and Allegro* for strings to Professor Sanford.

Still another honor awaited his return to England and this was specially dear to Elgar: Worcester presented him with the freedom of the city or in the American expression—"the key to the city." And as the procession marched to the Cathedral, with Elgar—gowned in his Doctor's robes—the center of attention, a man, old and feeble, looked down from a window high above the street and proudly answered the salute of his son!

A series of Birmingham lectures, a tour, and more honors took up the rest of 1905. Then in the following year after another trip to America, Elgar composed *The Kingdom,* intended as the second part of a series of oratorios of which the first was *The Apostles.* After that came a working-over of the music written years before for the children's play, *The Wand of Youth,* now divided into two suites of "children's music."

But it was not until the summer of 1908 that Elgar's creative urge again burst forth—this time in his first symphony. Though written within a period of a few months, it contained a lifetime of thought and experience. Hans Richter—to whom the symphony was dedicated—conducted its first performance on December 3, 1908, in Manchester. England now had her own classical symphonist!

In the summer of 1909 Elgar's mind returned to his violin concerto. Years before he had begun one, but dissatisfied with it, he had torn it up. This time all went well except that his second symphony demanded to be written at the same time. The concerto triumphed, however, and was given a brilliant performance on the 10th of November, 1910, with Fritz Kreisler as the solo-violinist.

The following year Elgar was commissioned to write music for the coronation services of King George V and Queen Mary; in May his second symphony was given its first performance at the London Musical Festival; and on the 17th of June he received the Order of Merit.

Falstaff, his next important work—based on episodes in the life of Shakespeare's famous character—Elgar frequently called his best orchestral composition. Begun while he was on a visit to Italy in the beginning of 1913, it was finished in the invigorating seaside air of North Wales and given its first performance at a Leeds Festival on October 2, 1913.

The new year was taken up with smaller pieces but in July of 1914 he went off on a holiday to Scotland—his mind astir with the third part of the oratorio trilogy. Alas, August saw the outbreak of the First World War and oratorio-writing was out of the question.

Hurrying home, Elgar threw himself into war relief work and during these sad years wrote little, not related to the war. *Carillon*, based on a patriotic poem; *Polonia*, written for a Polish Relief Fund; *The Spirit of England*, a choral and orchestral work consisting of three parts; a set of songs called *Fringes of the Fleet*, based on poems of Rudyard Kipling—all these, and many more war compositions poured from his pen.

Fortunately, during the summer of 1918 his mind turned to chamber music and he busied himself with three works at once: a violin sonata, a string quartet and a quintet for piano and strings. Written in the country, far removed from the horror of war, they all reflect a quality of calm and a

72

prophecy of peace. In addition to these, he also wrote a 'cello concerto which was given its first performance with Felix Salmond playing the solo part on October 27, 1919, at Queen's Hall. A certain sadness in this work unconsciously foretold a tragedy that befell Elgar the following spring: his wife, Caroline Alice Elgar, suddenly fell ill and died.

Gradually life returned to him and remembering some talks with Richard Strauss about orchestrating Bach's organ works, he began to orchestrate Bach's Fugue in C minor. This, together with his growing interest in the study of microscopes, filled his days and revived his spirit.

At the beginning of 1923 Elgar consented to write incidental music for Lawrence Binyon's play, *King Arthur;* and in 1924 he was made Master of King's Musick—a position he took very seriously indeed! Thereafter more honors poured in upon him; he busied himself with various orchestrations; the writing of incidental music to plays; and then wrote the *Nursery Suite,* which he dedicated to the Duchess of York and her two daughters, the Princesses Elizabeth and Margaret Rose.

In 1932 the British Broadcasting Company celebrated Elgar's seventy-fifth birthday with a three-concert festival during which they announced that they had commissioned him to write a third symphony. He set to work with new vigor and—as was his custom—his mind immediately sought something else to go hand in hand with the symphony. And having always wanted to write an opera, he decided to try once again. After various complications he set to work on his opera, *The Spanish Lady.*

Thus he worked—first on the symphony, then on the opera—equally excited about both of them. But destiny interferred with their completion. Elgar fell ill in the midst of his work and after a lingering illness, died on February 23, 1934, at Worcester.

Now as time goes on the world recognizes more and more the eminence of Edward Elgar—particularly in the field of orchestral music—who, like Falstaff, lives on—"for England and St. George!"

DELIUS

Courtesy of "Musical Courier"

FREDERICK DELIUS

Dreamer in Music

BORN 1862—DIED 1934

Frederick Delius—of Dutch-German parentage and destined to become a distinguished composer, living in France most of his mature life—was born on January 29, 1862, at Bradford, England. Thus it was that England gave birth within five years to two major composers—Edward Elgar and Frederick Delius.

Frederick was the fourth child in a family of fourteen. His father, Julius Delius, a prosperous wool merchant, ruled his home with an iron hand. And although both he and his wife, Elise Pauline, knew and enjoyed music they were horrified when their young son showed signs of taking music seriously. Frederick was, in fact, a problem in more ways than one to them. Once, having buried himself in highly improbable adventure stories, he ran away from home to seek his fortune; another time, fascinated by a circus performer's antics, he tried to imitate the act on his own horse—with sad results! Hurled from the horse and badly injured, he was forced to lie flat on his back for weeks.

And now this music idea! What was to be done with such a boy? True, he had taught himself to play the piano by ear, and later, his teachers had been impressed with his progress on the violin. But of what value was all this in the world of business? And to this world any son of Julius Delius belonged!

Accordingly, after first attending Frankland's School, then the Bradford

Grammar School and finally the International College at Isleworth—where he composed his first song—Frederick was taken into his father's woolen business. He was sent immediately to Chemnitz, Germany, to learn the business. While there he took violin lessons from Hans Sitt and heard a great deal of good music.

One night after hearing a stirring performance of Wagner's *The Mastersingers*, Delius said to himself, "I want to be a composer."

This decision did not, of course, make him one, but served to direct his course of action. Possessing the same headstrong tendency of his father —though in the opposite direction—Delius set his mind to work on a way of escape from the woolen business. Accordingly, after business-learning trips to France and the Scandinavian countries, and a winter spent in his uncle's office in Manchester, Delius mustered enough courage to go to his father with this proposition: "If I must be a business man let me be an orange planter in Florida."

"What next!" exclaimed Julius Delius.

But at the same time, thinking to himself that anything would be better than having an irresponsible musician in the family, he arranged to buy an orange plantation for his son.

Thus in the spring of 1884, Frederick Delius found himself in escape from the world, traveling a three days' journey from Jacksonville, Florida, along the St. John's River to his newly acquired plantation, Solano Grove. Having been fascinated by maps of America since he was a boy, he had now picked Florida as looking both remote and peaceful. And since to satisfy his father's code of life, he must have some occupation, he had hit upon orange-growing as a promise of both profit and romance!

Arrived at Solano Grove, he was the only white man in a world as remote in feeling as a spot on the moon. It was exactly what he had longed for; and once he had transferred the running of the plantation to an overseer, he settled down to a dream life, surrounded by singing colored folk: spending his time afloat in a canoe, strolling in the sweet-scented woods in the evening, and above all—thinking, musing, coming of age in his own spirit.

Meanwhile, having kept up his violin practice, he eventually felt the need for further outlet of his music-learning. He must have a piano. Accordingly, he made the long trip to Jacksonville to select one and arrange for its shipment to Solano.

As he tried one instrument in the Jacksonville music shop his unusual improvising attracted the attention of a fellow-customer, Thomas F. Ward, a Jacksonville organist, formerly from Brooklyn, now living in Florida for his health. They liked each other at once. Each was stimulated by the other's approach to music: the result being, that Thomas Ward accepted an invitation from Delius to take a vacation and spend six months at Solano Grove. In return for his holiday Ward taught Delius harmony and counterpoint, and in later years, Delius often declared, "Ward was my only *teacher* worth the name."

At the end of six months, Delius *knew* that his life belonged to music. And after repeated unsuccessful attempts to convince his father by letter of this, Delius took the matter into his own hands, gave up the plantation and went to Jacksonville where he made his living by teaching and singing in a Jewish Synagogue.

Later, with glowing letters of introduction from his Jacksonville friends, and with one dollar in his pocket, he arrived in Danville, Virginia, where he taught literature and music with unique success at the Roanoke Female School. Within a year he went on to New York City where he earned his living as an organist.

Finally, in June 1886, Julius Delius relented and gave his son an allowance which permitted him to carry out his long hoped-for wish to study at the Leipzig Conservatory. Delius went to·Leipzig in August of that year and studied under Hans Sitt, Salomon Jadassohn and Karl Reinecke.

The following summer while on a walking tour through Norway, he met the famous composer Edvard Grieg and this proved to be more than a casual acquaintance. Visiting Leipzig the following winter, Grieg had the opportunity of hearing at the Conservatory the first performance of a Delius work —the *Florida* suite. Convinced of the young man's ability, Grieg took it upon himself to visit Julius Delius on his next trip to England. And Grieg's reputation as a composer won the day for Delius. His father reluctantly consented, upon Grieg's persuasion, to give his son a small allowance and best of all, he promised not to interfere with his musical career.

Delius went immediately to Paris where a sympathetic uncle provided him with an increased income. For a time he lived at Croissy, France. Then in 1890, he settled in Paris where he began to compose music in a style peculiarly his own: stimulated by the company of such artists as the dramatist, Strindberg; the painter, Gauguin; and musicians, Maurice Ravel and Florent Schmitt.

During this period he composed: *Seven Norwegian Songs;* a tone poem, *Sur les cemes*—his first work to be given a public performance; a violin sonata, a string quartet and an opera *The Magic Fountain:* the tone poem *Over the Hills and Far Away* and *Two Verlaine Songs.*

Then came an opera, *Koanga,* and the first version of his *Appalachia* variations, a work that had been conceived while he was still in Florida. At about this time he met an unusual woman, Jelka Rosen, who was both a painter and a poet. She was immediately attracted to this young poet-musician, and invited him to visit her mother at Grez-sur-Loing, a suburb of Paris, where Delius soon came to feel very much at home.

In 1897 after a hurried trip to Florida—a gesture to a dream—he returned to France, married Jelka Rosen and eventually settled with her in a sprawling house at Grez-sur-Loing; and with a wife whom he worshipped, began to express his deepest emotions in music.

One other factor contributed to his maturity—his discovery of the philosopher Friedrich Nietzsche. Delius felt strangely drawn to the thoughts of this poet-philosopher who had been both friend and foe to Richard Wagner; and he eventually composed a great choral work, *A Mass of Life,* based on Nietzsche's *Also Spake Zarathustra.*

Meanwhile in 1899 Delius composed an orchestral work, *Paris: The song of a Great City,* which was first performed and appreciated in Germany. Then during the next two years he worked on a truly remarkable opera, *A Village Romeo and Juliet.* In it he attempted to have his music express the story. In a way, he intended it to be a symphonic poem in reverse—the action on the stage *dramatizing* the music. It, also, was given its first performance in Germany; then finally in London under Sir Thomas Beecham who became one of Delius's strongest supporters and finest interpreters.

Margot La Rouge, another opera followed: then a revision of his *Appalachia,* and in 1903 a delicate choral work, *Sea Drift,* inspired by Walt Whitman's poem. During 1904 and 1905 he was busy with *A Mass of Life* which he always considered his finest work. After that came an entirely different phase in a set of songs called *Songs at Sunset* and a work inspired by the poet, Ernest Dawson, *Cynara* for baritone and orchestra.

Then in 1907 began what was still another phase—the purely orchestral one—which included: *Brigg Fair,* the first *Dance Rhapsody, In a Summer Garden, Summer Night on the River* and *On Hearing the First Cuckoo in Spring.*

Strangely enough, these pieces arouse a deeper feeling of the English countryside than many a composition, composed by Englishmen residing on English soil. It is an inner essence that Delius expressed in sound such as Renoir, the painter, succeeded in doing for the French people in color.

At the beginning of the World War Delius and his wife buried their silver and other valued possessions in the yard at Grez-sur-Loing and fled to England. There Delius composed his Second Violin Sonata, Requiem, Concerto for violin and cello and orchestra, and Violin concerto, Dance Rhapsody, No. 2, a string quartet, *A Song Before Sunrise* and various other works.

Back at Grez-sur-Loing Delius composed incidental music for Flecker's oriental play, *Hassan,* and a cello concerto. In 1922 he began to show signs of a serious illness; by 1924 he was partially paralyzed and in 1926 he became totally blind and dependent upon others for his every move. This was a sore trial for a man of Delius's independent and sensitive nature, but in time, with the help of his wife, he adjusted himself to a new way of life.

Meanwhile though ill, he had attended a performance of *A Mass of Life* at Wiesbaden, Germany; and he had received one of the few honors ever to come his way—the gold medal of the London Philharmonic Society.

Then it so happened that a young musician by the name of Eric Fenby—born in Yorkshire, the section of England from which Delius came—after long thought, wrote to Delius offering his services as amanuensis. In other

81

words, he would live at the Delius home and take down what the composer dictated, edit music and generally make himself useful. Delius accepted the offer.

Thus in 1928 began one of the most unique relationships in musical history. After a few trials and errors Fenby learned, by a kind of spiritual telepathy, to understand the sick man's intentions, and he eventually put many of Delius's early works in shape and set down some new ones.

Despite the devotion displayed towards Delius by the discriminating few, he was still relatively unsung in his native England, but in 1929, due to the efforts of Sir Thomas Beecham, a six-concert Delius Festival was held in London. With great effort, Delius, in the company of his wife and Eric Fenby, attended these concerts: sitting sightless there on the platform, but keenly alert to the genuine response to his music.

Meanwhile shortly before the Festival he had given Fenby his gold watch and chain; for the young man, under trying circumstances, had become genuinely dear to him. Working together off and on after the Festival, they completed several works—the last one being an *Idyll* for soprano, baritone and orchestra, completed in 1933.

Delius died at Grez-sur-Loing on June 10, 1934, with the wish that he be buried in an English village near a church "Where the winds are warm and the sun friendly."

And the year after his death his body was removed to such a spot at Limpsfield, England. To the strains of his own music, conducted by Sir Thomas Beecham, he was buried beneath an ancient wind-whipped tree. But the spirit of Delius lives—dream-like—in music outside and above the craftsman's world; in music that captures and instills an impression through magically woven harmonies into something we recognize as Delius.

STRAUSS

RICHARD STRAUSS

Story-Teller in Music

BORN 1864

Sixty years after the birth of Johann Strauss, known as "The Father of the Waltz," and nearly forty years after the birth of Johann Strauss, Jr., "The Waltz-King," on June 11, 1864, at Munich, another Strauss—destined to become famous in the world of music—was born. He was named Richard by his father, Franz Strauss, who was a leading horn-player in the Munich Opera and not a member of the Waltz-Strauss family.

Richard began life not only with a silver spoon in his mouth—for his mother Josephine Pschorr came from a wealthy brewing family—but with the gods of talent in generous attendance.

As a small child—to the great delight of his musician-father—he displayed genuine musical ability. When he was four years old he began to study music with a court harpist by the name of August Tombs. At six he composed his first piece of music—a polka, as well as a Christmas Song.

Surely a boy with this much talent should have every advantage. Accordingly, in his eighth year he began to study violin with Benno Walter, leader of the Munich Court Orchestra; and by the time he was eleven he was deep in the study of composition and instrumentation with the musical director, F. W. Meyer.

Meanwhile piano pieces, songs, sonatas, and overtures poured forth with slight effort. And when upon occasion, friends of Franz Strauss whispered, half in awe, "He is another Mozart," Richard's father was happy indeed; for

85

it was his dearest wish that his son would carry on the classical tradition.

Little did he know how far Richard would stray from that path before he unconsciously struggled back to it, too late to shed freshness there.

The first private performance of a work by this promising young man occurred while he was still a student at the Gymnasium, or high school; and in 1881 when he was only seventeen, Hermann Levi, the famous Wagnerian conductor, presided over Richard Strauss's first symphony! The following year his *Serenade* for wind instruments was conducted by Franz Wullner; Levi then gave his concert overture in C minor; his violin teacher Benno Walter played in his violin concerto; and in 1884 before young Strauss was twenty-one years old, his music had been introduced to America by Theodore Thomas who conducted his Symphony in F minor for the New York Philharmonic Society.

Meanwhile the young composer had been attending University classes where he studied philosophy and the fine arts. But in 1883, finding formal school life dull beside the dazzling prospects of a musical career, he gave up his University studies and went to Berlin for the winter where good fortune waved her customary wand in his direction. Straight off, the eminent conductor, Hans von Bülow, became interested in this remarkable young fellow and made him assistant conductor at Meiningen the following October. And then one month later, upon Bülow's resignation, Strauss found himself Hofkapellmeister, or musical director!

Although he held this position only until the following April, this period proved a turning point in his career; for it so happened that a member of the orchestra—Alexander Ritter, thirty years his senior and as enthusiastic over the music of Liszt and Wagner as young Strauss's father was against it—succeeded in turning the budding composer away from the traditional forms of Brahms and Schumann to the more colorful music of Liszt, Berlioz and Wagner.

Filled with the spirit of this new sound world, Strauss went, in the spring of 1886, to Italy—a journey which resulted in his symphonic fantasy, *Aus Italien*. But even with such amazing musical tools as he had at his disposal, he could not capture the spirit of a people that easily: *Aus Italien* proved the merest indication towards the road of the symphonic poem that he was to follow.

Returning to his native land in late summer, Strauss became third-conductor at the Munich Opera. And during the next three years—his official duties being light—he composed three of his first characteristic works. These were the stories in music, or symphonic poems: *Macbeth, Don Juan,* and *Death and Transfiguration.*

In the autumn of 1889, he resigned from his Munich position and went to Weimar as conductor at the Court Opera. Weimar was the city to which Liszt had introduced the music of Richard Wagner and other composers in their struggling stage long before the world had recognized them. And it was during the five years that Strauss stayed there that he laid the foundation of his own dazzling success as a composer.

Greatly overworked, Strauss fell seriously ill in 1892. Consequently, he went on an extended trip that winter and the following spring, through Greece, Egypt and Sicily. During this time he not only regained his health but wrote most of his first opera, *Guntram.* It was, in fact, a music drama, written in the style of Richard Wagner. Like Wagner he wrote the text as well as the music, but unlike Wagner he was neither sufficiently steeped in his subject nor equipped with enough inner emotion to produce more than an imitation of his model.

Guntram was finished the following year in Weimar and was given its first production there in May, 1894, with Strauss conducting. Although only moderately successful this production was of special significance to Strauss, for Pauline de Ahna who created the leading role of Freihild became his wife on September 10th of that year. A singer of unusual intelligence, she became a noted interpreter of her husband's songs and proved to be a genuine help-mate in his work.

Meanwhile his reputation was growing by leaps and bounds: Cosima Wagner invited him to Bayreuth to conduct *Tannhäuser;* in the fall of 1894 he was recalled to Munich as Court Conductor, and a few months later he succeeded Hans von Bülow—who had recently died—as conductor of the Berlin Philharmonic Concerts.

87

In addition to these strenuous duties Strauss found time to compose one major symphonic poem during each of the following four years. The year 1895 produced *Till Eulenspiegel* which relates in music the merry pranks of a practical jokester. In the following year came *Thus Spake Zarathustra*, described by Strauss as a musical tribute to the genius of the German philosopher Frederick Nietzsche; *Don Quixote*, based on the Cervantes novel, was completed in 1897; and then came *Ein Heldenleben*, or *A Hero's Life*, the hero generally regarded to be Strauss.

After five years he composed the symphonic work, *Sinfonia domestica*, or *Domestic Symphony*, which, in a way, carries on the story of *A Hero's Life*. And having become famous both as conductor and composer, he was invited to America in the spring of 1904, where, on the 21st of March he conducted the first performance of this work.

Sinfonia domestica closed one period of his career. Strauss had then reached the limit of descriptive music without the help of words; and opera was the natural result. *Feuersnot*, his second opera, begun in 1899, had been given its first performance on November 21, 1901, at Dresden. And before *Sinfonia domestica* was entirely finished, *Salome*, based on the play by Oscar Wilde, was under way. This opera was given its first performance at Dresden on December 9, 1905. Daring in subject matter and unusual in treatment, it burst upon the musical world like a bomb shell.

Soon after the first performance of *Salome*, Strauss began the composition of *Electra*. The libretto or story to the opera was written by Hugo von Hofmannstahl who eventually provided Strauss with six opera stories and one ballet story. *Electra*, based on the ancient Greek legend, tells a story of horror realistically in music. And the reception to its first performance at Dresden on January 25, 1909, was even more sensational than that of *Salome*.

Then Strauss began work on an entirely different opera, *Der Rosenkavalier* or *The Rose Cavalier*, again to a story of Hugo von Hofmannstahl. This tragi-comic story, very dear to the heart of Strauss, awakened in him his deep-seated love of Mozart. The result—though not blessed with Mozart's child-like purity of humor—is one of the world's most delightful operas, and is sometimes known as the "Waltz-opera."

Following *Der Rosenkavalier* Strauss wrote eight operas and two ballets, but his reputation in the opera world still rests with *Salome, Electra* and *Der Rosenkavalier*.

Throughout his career Strauss composed many songs, but only a few of them are generally known. These include: *Cäcilie, Morgen* and *Traum durch die Dämmerung*.

Meanwhile various official positions occupied his time in addition to the great amount of composing and the conducting of his own works in various places, including a second trip to America in 1922 for that purpose. From 1898 until 1918 he was conductor of the Royal Opera in Berlin; in 1908 he was made General Musical Director, and in 1910 he became a member of the Akademie der Künste in Berlin. He had charge of a master-class for composition at the Berlin Hochschule für Musik from 1917 until 1920; and in 1919 he became co-director of the Vienna State Opera.

During the five years that he held this position he divided his time between Vienna—where he lived in a large mansion, built on land granted him by the state—and his country estate in Garmisch, Bavaria.

In the fall of 1933, Strauss was appointed president of the Reichs-Musik-kammer in Berlin, but he resigned in the spring of 1935 and retired to Garmisch. While visiting London as guest-conductor in 1937 he was awarded the gold medal of the Philharmonic Society—this being only one of the many honors bestowed upon him during his career.

Richard Strauss, the most famous German composer of his generation, stands today as the master performer in composition, the manipulator of instruments, and the story-teller in music.

SIBELIUS

Courtesy of "Musical Courier"

JEAN SIBELIUS

"Symphonist of the North"

BORN 1865

On DECEMBER 8, 1865, at Tavastehus in the little northern country of Finland, a son was born to Dr. Christian Gustaf Sibelius and his wife Maria Carlotta. He was named Johan Julian Christian; as a child he was called Janne by his playmates and today the world knows him as Jean Sibelius.

His father, who was a greatly loved doctor and surgeon, contracted typhus fever from one of his patients and died when Janne was but two and a half years old. Left alone with three small children, Maria Carlotta Sibelius set about to make their lives as happy as possible to offset the lack of a father. And in this respect, she was helped by both the children's grandmothers.

In later years Sibelius remembered his Grandmother Catharina Juliana Borg as stricter than his Grandmother Catharina Fredrika Sibelius; but there was a logical reason for this. The fatherless Sibelius family lived with Grandmother Borg during the school year when discipline was necessary; while at vacation time, off they went to Grandmother Sibelius's home in Lovisa—or the islands nearby—where they had the most wonderful time. Grandmother Sibelius and their Aunt Evelina tried their best to be cross at some of the impish pranks of their summer guests, but somehow, their scolding always resulted in laughter on both sides.

Grandmother Sibelius and Aunt Evelina took particular delight in young Janne's buoyant spirits and marveled at his love of roaming the woods—together with his special quality of at-homeness with nature. Best of all, they

93

saw the spark of music developing in him and being musical themselves, they encouraged the boy in that direction.

Janne began to take piano lessons when he was nine years old. From the first, he was no ordinary pupil. Sitting at the piano, he would make up tunes for hours at a time and some of them he remembered well enough, later, to whistle to the birds as he roamed about in the woods. When he was ten years old he wrote his first real composition—*Drops of Water*—written for violin and violoncello.

"It really *does* sound like drops of water!" whispered Aunt Evelina to Janne's grandmother.

"So it does. So it does," admitted Catharina Fredrika Sibelius, "but we must be cautious about over-praising him. First of all he must get a sound classical education."

Be it as it may, the next composition to appear from the promising young northern composer was in the form of program music, a story of "Aunt Evelina's Life in Music."

In addition to all these loving female relatives, an uncle whose name was Pehr or Peter Sibelius played an important part in young Janne's life. He was a successful business man whose leisure hours were devoted to music and astronomy. As a matter of fact, he had a habit of playing his violin around two o'clock in the morning when every-day folk were fast asleep. He too, encouraged Janne in his love for music but at the same time advised his young nephew to follow in his footsteps and take up the study of astronomy as a profession.

Still another uncle influenced the future composer's life in a most peculiar way. He was Uncle Johan, eldest son in Janne's father's family, who when a very young man had gone away to sea. Two years before Janne's birth he had died of yellow fever in Havana; but Janne felt that he knew his sailor-uncle through having read a trunk full of his letters. And coming one day upon a package of calling cards, bearing the French form of his Uncle's name, Jean Sibelius, Janne made a great decision:

"I shall become Jean Sibelius."

Carefully packing the cards away, he used them as his own when he became a young student in Helsingfors, and as we know, he gradually brought the name *Jean Sibelius* into being!

Meanwhile in 1876—the year made famous in musical history by the first performance of the complete *Ring of the Nibelung* at Bayreuth—Janne was sent to a splendid school, the Hamman Lyseo of Tavastland. This school represented the highest form of Finnish culture and through its influence Janne became interested in the famous national epic poem, the *Kalevala,* as well as Scandinavian myths, and the classical works of Homer and Horace.

Finland had striven, first, to throw off the cultural domination of Sweden, then, that of Russia. She was just emerging with a culture of her own and though Janne's ancestors possessed a mixture of Swedish blood through intermarriage, Janne was completely "Finnish" in spirit and responded heart and soul to his school's love of country.

No one subject interested him more than another, until, as he approached the age of fifteen, music took complete possession of him. He began to study the violin with Gustaf Levander, Tavastehus military band leader. He would be a violinist! He would be a great violinist! And this ambition remained with him for ten years.

Soon he was playing the violin for various school affairs; then as his skill developed he organized a trio in his own home—with his sister Linda playing the piano; his brother Christian playing the violoncello and he, Janne, acting both as violinist and conductor!

In the beginning the trio played, chiefly, the works of Mozart, Haydn and Beethoven. This had the effect of both grounding the young composer in the classical tradition and inspiring him to learn the laws and rules of musical theory. Searching one day through the school library, he had the good fortune to come upon a copy of a famous book on musical composition by Adolph Bernhard Marx. Setting about the task of studying it by himself, he soon mastered the theory of musical construction and became familiar with the various musical forms.

His own composing began to benefit from this new knowledge, but none of his many compositions of that time possess the individual quality that we have come to recognize as Sibelius. Only one characteristic, of those associated with his mature music, appeared in these early efforts—his love of nature! The pungent smell of burning hemp, or the shimmering pools of melting ice gently announcing the approach of spring after a cold winter, could be plainly *heard* by one of his boyhood friends as Janne improvised at the piano.

But soon it was time to think of weightier matters than tune-making.

"Janne, you cannot possibly think of following music as a career!" exclaimed Grandmother Borg in horror.

He not only *thought* of it, but he was possessed with music above everything else. Reminded by his mother, however, of how much he, his brother and sister owed to their grandmother, he could not deny her the pleasure of seeing him enrolled as a law student at the University of Helsingfors. But his interest in music was too genuine a thing to be snuffed out by a sense of duty: on September 15, 1885, he also enrolled at the musical academy as a special student. And a story that he later told on himself explains how he eventually followed the career of his choice.

He had borrowed a certain history book, prescribed in one of his classes, from a friend. Having read a few pages without much interest he put it down for the moment, open where he had stopped reading it, on the window sill. Several months later an uncle happened to visit him and when he saw the open book with its pages grown yellow from long exposure to the sun, he turned to his nephew and said, "If study does not interest you any more than this, perhaps you *should* devote your time to music."

Thus it was that with this amount of encouragement, Janne made up his mind to be a musician. And when he returned to Helsingfors in the fall, after his summer holiday, he definitely deserted law for music. Still hoping to be a violinist, he specialized in the violin under a noted teacher by the name of Csillag and, at first, studied musical theory, merely as a supplementary subject.

Fortunately, the head of the musical academy, Martin Wegelius, a man of unusual perception, recognized an unawakened genius in Sibelius. Realizing that he was dealing with a strong, individual spirit, Wegelius was doubly careful to direct his young student along sound, basic lines of theory, harmony and counterpoint. Despite this strict discipline, teacher and pupil—separated by twenty years' difference in age—became fast friends.

Sibelius spent a large share of his summer vacations at the Wegelius home on Fir Island. This was of enormous benefit to him. In the mornings he worked diligently at his counterpoint studies; Wegelius and he played sonatas together in the afternoon; and then the day usually ended with Mrs. Wegelius serving refreshments while they all sat listening to her husband read aloud to them.

Wegelius, a man of great culture, was chiefly interested in literature and the history of civilization. In music, he favored the German school and considered Richard Wagner the shining star in that world.

Sibelius, on the other hand, stubbornly held to a preference for the music of Grieg, Tchaikovsky and even that of Brahms—which was particularly distasteful to Wegelius because of Brahms's rivalry with Wagner.

Fortunately, pupil and teacher respected each other's opinion enough to cause no ill effects in their relationship, though it must be admitted that for some time Sibelius led a double life. As a pupil—realizing their value—he conscientiously carried out the rules of his teacher. As a composer—he was in secret—writing music in his own language. A violin sonata, written during the winter of 1886-87, and shared with very few, revealed a remarkable freshness of inspiration and treatment. A piano trio, written the following summer, also foretold an individual talent.

But Wegelius must have known *something* about his pupil's secret composing, for in the spring of 1888, he asked Sibelius to collaborate with him in writing the music to a dramatic fairy tale, *The Watersprite*, to be given for a special occasion at the musical academy. Thus his portion of the music called "The Watersprite's Song" remains a landmark in his career for this music, played at the academy performance on April 9, 1888, introduced Sibelius to the world as a composer.

Shortly afterward he was represented at an academy recital by a *Theme and Variations* in C sharp minor for string quartet. But now after administering three years of discipline, Wegelius realized that he must give Sibelius more freedom to develop his individual talent. And the result came in two highly original works with which Sibelius finished his career at the academy. One was a string suite in A major for violin, viola and violoncello, performed on April 13, 1889, and the other was a string quartet in A minor, performed on May 29, 1889.

Meanwhile an unusually gifted composer-pianist, Ferruccio Busoni, had been lured to Helsingsfors to teach piano; and although Sibelius was not one of his pupils, the two had become staunch friends. Completely opposite in temperament—Busoni being a product of the city and wholly unable to share Sibelius's love of country and nature—they, nevertheless, met on musical grounds. Busoni was particularly enthusiastic over Sibelius's string trio and looked forward to the quartet. When it was finished, he sat down at the piano and played the score directly through at sight, in marvelous fashion. He immediately recognized the genuine ability revealed in this composition and thenceforth, until his early death in 1924, contributed in a practical way toward making Sibelius's music known to an appreciative world.

Another important figure at the conclusion of Sibelius's academy days was the foremost Finnish music critic, Karl Flodin. On many occasions he had talked with the young composer at a favorite café where kindred spirits met, but not until he heard these "graduation" compositions was he fully aware of Sibelius's musical ability. He was, in fact, astonished; and predicted a great future for Sibelius.

A scholarship, followed by a government grant resulted from these evidences of extraordinary talent. Thus Sibelius went with his mother, brother and sister to Lovisa that summer with a light heart. In the fall he was going to the big outside world of music—to Berlin, one of its very centers!

Meanwhile he spent a lazy summer. Twenty-three years old, tall, attractive, and unusually intelligent, he was frequently coaxed into the social life of Lovisa. But what a figure he made playing the piano for dancing!

"No, Janne—not that way—it's too slow." Or, "How can we dance when you play such beautiful things that we just have to stop and listen?"

Though on a vacation, music tormented him constantly. On one occasion when his mother was serving tea to some ladies in the drawing room, the door suddenly opened, a young man clad in a short shirt entered, walked directly to the piano and began to play, unaware that there was anyone in the room.

"Janne!" exclaimed his mother.

And as the tea cups clanked in their saucers, an embarrassed young composer came to life and dashed for cover.

September came at last and Sibelius, in the company of some good friends, started off by steamer for Lübeck on the way to Berlin. Martin Wegelius bade him God-speed and it was an excited young man, indeed, who waved good-by as the steamer pulled away from shore.

Berlin was not all that he had expected, but nothing could have lived up to his imagination at that period. At least he had an opportunity of hearing good music played by large orchestras; he became entranced by the piano playing of Hans von Bülow, particularly his interpretation of the Beethoven sonatas; he had the opportunity of hearing Richard Strauss's tone poem, Don Juan, on an occasion when Strauss—a year older than he—was in the audience; and he studied faithfully with Albert Becker, a noted theory teacher. At times the eternal putting-together of fugues for Herr Becker irked the ambitious young composer but in later years he was grateful for this training.

And as a matter of fact, when Sibelius mustered enough courage to show his teacher the manuscript of his piano quintette in G minor, written in Berlin during this strict fugue training period, Becker was deeply moved. Although it was not in the strict style of his pupil's lesson, it was authentic and he could not conceal his pleasure in it.

This Berlin period amounted to a finding-of-himself. He often sat talking way into the night with congenial friends about music, literature, art and life. At other times he would sit at the piano improvising for his friends by the hour. And during this time he met, for the first time, Robert Kajanus, the noted Finnish conductor and composer, who was greatly responsible for firing Sibelius's interest in the Finnish epic, Kalevala.

With the coming of spring, he returned to Finland for a vacation and during his stay there, spent some time with a family by the name of Järnefelt whose company he greatly enjoyed. In fact, by autumn of that year he was

99

engaged to Aino Järnefelt. Both families were delighted. It was fine to see Janne settling down! And General Järnefelt, a strict Finnish patriot of great culture, saw possibilities of originality and greatness in this hearty young man and welcomed him as a future son-in-law.

Vacation over, Sibelius set out for Vienna as one more step in his education. Arrived there, he found the Austrian city—just as Berlin had been—divided into two camps of loyalty: one on the side of Brahms and one on the side of Wagner. Sibelius, true to his inner nature, joined neither, though he met Brahms in person at a café one evening; and sought advice from Hans Richter, the noted Wagnerian conductor. On Richter's advice, he studied orchestration with Robert Fuchs, a staunch Brahms' follower; and through an introduction from Martin Wegelius, he became a special pupil of the composer, Karl Goldmark.

But though steeped in the Viennese atmosphere, and tutored by "foreign" teachers, Sibelius remained the northern composer. It was during that winter, in fact, that he made the first draft of his *Kullervo*, based on a myth in the Finnish *Kalevala;* and some of the themes for his highly original *En Saga* came into being in Vienna.

He loved Vienna—its gaiety, its laughter, its music! Johann Strauss, Jr., a man of sixty-five, was conducting his own waltzes and the atmosphere of Beethoven, Mozart and Schubert hovered fondly over the city. Through it all sauntered Sibelius, gloriously drinking it in, but emerging—Jean Sibelius, the graduate, going home to Finland in the spring of 1891—ready to face a career of work and integrity.

After an idle summer spent with his family at Lovisa, he settled down there in the fall and winter in order to finish the works he had begun in Vienna. Occasionally, for the sake of intellectual refreshment, he went to Helsingfors for a few days where he divided his time between the Järnefelt family and a group of young authors, painters and musicians whose enthusiasm for creative work was particularly inspiring to Sibelius. He always returned to Lovisa, fired with a desire to contribute to Finnish culture and more eager than ever to accomplish good work.

Thus it was under these favorable circumstances that *Kullervo*, his first major composition, was completed. This symphonic poem, given its first performance on April 28, 1892, met with immediate success and provided proof that he was justified in following an artistic career.

Accordingly, on June 10, 1892, he and Aino Järnefelt were married. His bride, coming from a Finnish family of unusual culture and refinement, enriched his life and contributed greatly to his artistic growth. They spent the summer in Karelia on the shore of Lake Pielisjärvi. Sibelius was fascinated with the folk-music of the Karelian countryside, and curiously enough, had captured their sound-language in his *Kullervo* before ever having heard them sing. Instead of using actual Finnish folk-tunes, he had drawn upon the "Finnish" within himself and thus produced authentic Finnish music.

During the summer he composed three songs to words by the poet, Runeberg, and adding these to some earlier ones, he had them published in the fall of 1892, under the title, *Seven Songs by Runeberg*.

Life now became an earnest matter for Sibelius. Moving to Helsingfors in the fall, he began to teach theory at the musical academy; he played second violin in the academy string quartet and he taught theory in the orchestra school of the Philharmonic Society. His good friend, Robert Kojanus, had arranged this last position to increase Sibelius's income, and he contributed then and later towards making Sibelius's music known to the public.

"Write something that I can put in the orchestra's regular repertory," suggested Kojanus. "Something that the people, hearing again and again, will understand and like."

And the result was the brilliant orchestral piece, *En Saga*, not the simple piece that Kojanus had in mind, perhaps, but at least one worthy of having been fostered.

The following summer Sibelius began work on an opera based on a Kalevala subject. The opera never materialized but the subject appeared later in his *Lemminkäinen* suite. Before he could get to that, however, he busied himself with his *Karelia* suite, written for a series of historical tableaux.

At the end of the season Sibelius took a trip to Italy, where he visited Rome, Venice and other southern cities, becoming thoroughly enchanted with the country. From Italy he went to Bayreuth to meet his brother-in-law,

Armas Järnefelt, an ardent Wagnerian. But although Sibelius heard fine performances of *Tannhäuser* and *Lohengrin,* he could not be persuaded to remain for the rest of the Wagner festival. Somehow, he could not be won over to Wagner's music, and perhaps this was natural. Possessed of so much originality of his own, he instinctively avoided influences of any kind.

At the same time, eager to be about his work, he went to Munich for a month where he busied himself with the *Lemminkäinen* suite. And back home once more, this *Kalevala* suite continued to occupy the greater share of his creative hours, outside his musical academy duties. The *Lemminkäinen* suite or cycle—consisting of four tone poems—*Lemminkäinen and the Maidens, Lemminkäinen in Tuonela, The Swan of Tuonela* and *The Return of Lemminkäinen*—was completed at the beginning of 1896 and performed for the first time in April of that year. They were later revised and *The Swan of Tuonela* has become the most popular one.

In 1897 the Finnish Government voted to allow Sibelius an annual grant of about four hundred dollars. While this was not sufficient to permit him to devote all his time to composing, it helped considerably. And although it was necessary for him to continue his teaching at the musical academy, this was not wasted time, by any means, for he was an excellent teacher. He possessed the special ability of transmitting his own enthusiasm to others and he was able, with the fewest possible words, to convey his meaning. One of his favorite expressions was, "See that there are no dead notes in a composition." And surely every note *lives* in his music.

The closing years of the century saw Sibelius started on a new and major phase of his career; for it was on April 26, 1899, that his first symphony was introduced at an all-Sibelius concert. At this same concert appeared his stirring *Song of the Athenians,* and both of these compositions proclaimed to the world Sibelius's affiliation with Finland's struggle for independence from Russian domination.

But it was in the fall of that year that his name became one with Finland. At the end of a series of historical tableaux, given at a patriotic celebration, came a stirring piece of music by Sibelius. It announced to the world: "We are a free people. We will fight for our rights. We are Finland!" Because of its revolutionary character, its true name was not used until later. At various times it was called: *Suomi, Vaterland,* and *La Patri,* but today it is known the world over as *Finlandia.*

Despite these various triumphs, Sibelius was still comparatively unknown outside Finland. But this was all changed in the summer of 1900 when he went with the Helsingfors Philharmonic Orchestra on its tour through various European cities, ending in great triumph at the Paris Exhibition. His music had now spoken outside his native land and this was just the beginning of its journey!

Having made arrangements for a substitute to take charge of his musical academy classes, in the fall of 1900, Sibelius took his family abroad—stopping first in Berlin for several months. One splendid thing after another came his way; and one in particular, was of great importance. While attending a reception at the house of Otto Lessmans, publisher of the famous *Allgemeine Musik Zeitung,* Sibelius permitted some of his songs to be sung by a Finnish soloist. The result was amazing. Richard Strauss happened to be among the guests and a few weeks later, to Sibelius's great surprise, he was informed that he was to be included among the composers at the famous Allgemeiner Deutscher Musikverein in Heidelberg. An honor indeed! For this society—founded forty years before by Franz Liszt and now completely under the control of Richard Strauss—favored, mostly, German composers.

Heartened by this recognition, Sibelius went southward with his family to Rapallo, Italy. And there in the midst of hills, bursting with blooming trees and flowers, his second symphony—unmistakably Sibelius-music-of-the-North but with the southern sun's radiance in it—came into being.

In May the Sibelius family started homeward by way of Prague where Sibelius was introduced to Antonin Dvořák by the latter's son-in-law, Joseph Suk. Then when they had scarcely arrived in Finland, it was time to start for the music festival in Heidelberg.

Arrived there, Sibelius felt doubtful about the concert at which he was to conduct *The Swan of Tuonela* and *The Return of Lemminkäinen.* In addition to lack of rehearsals, he was faced with the prospect of being sandwiched in between Richard Wagner and Richard Strauss on the program!

But despite these handicaps, the originality of his music plus his dynamic conducting won the day. Called before the audience again and again, he was hailed as one of the Great Ones!

Back home in Finland, Sibelius spent the summer at a seaside place, called Tvärminne, where some of his loveliest songs were written, including: *Was It a Dream? On a Balcony by the Sea,* and *Autumn Night.* And it was during that fall that his popular *Valse Triste* was written, first for strings only and later for a small orchestra.

Then he became absorbed in work on his violin concerto. Completed in its first form in the summer of 1903, it went through various changes before appearing in its final version—one that is regarded today as unique in its combination of "virtuoso" and artistic qualities.

Meanwhile a feeling of dissatisfaction had possessed Sibelius. While many other composers were seeking new methods, new techniques, new materials with which to express themselves in music, Sibelius was looking for the truth within himself. Finally, faced with the realization that city life dulled the fountain of his inspiration, in the spring of 1904, he decided to move into the country.

Having made up his mind, he set about at once to find a place, and he decided upon some property in Tomasby, about two miles from Järvenpää north of Helsingfors. That summer the Sibeliuses lived at a farmhouse nearby and watched their new home as it grew, log by log, from a stone foundation in the woods. They moved into it in September and within the mouth, Sibelius announced to a friend, "I have begun my third symphony."

Gradually his music found its way out into the world. At the beginning of 1905 Busoni invited him to Berlin to conduct his second symphony at one of the Moderne Musik concerts. The result was sensational: the strength, brilliance and imagination of his music won acclaim from both press and public. In the spring Granville Bantock conducted his first symphony, *Finlandia* and the *King Christian* suite in England with immense success; and at the same time Arturo Toscanini conducted *Finlandia* and *The Swan of Tuonela* in Italy. Sibelius had now definitely taken his place in the music world.

In the spring of 1905 he wrote his music for Maeterlinck's play, *Pelleas and Melisande*; that fall he went to England to conduct his second symphony at Liverpool; then home by way of Paris, and work on his third symphony, interspersed with the beginnings of his large symphonic work, based again on a Kalevala subject, *Pahjola's Daughter*. This was given its first performance under his leadership, shortly before Christmas, 1906, in St. Petersburg.

His third symphony was finished in the summer of 1907 and the following February, Sibelius, carrying out a long-cherished wish, went to London to conduct it at the Philharmonic Society. Back home, he suffered for a time from a serious throat ailment that contributed to a short period of depression. Doubts about life; doubts about his choice of career; financial worries piled up—then found release in his quartet, *Voces Intimae*. Following this confession-of-doubt in music, Sibelius began to compose with renewed energy: songs, tone-poems and piano pieces. And finally, in the spring of 1910, he started work on his truly remarkable fourth symphony.

Despite political unrest in his country and throughout the world, Sibelius buried himself in this symphony. Always reluctant to discuss a work not finished, he could not resist mentioning this one—"The symphony is breaking forth in sunshine and strength." Finished in the spring of 1911, this fourth symphony does indeed breathe "sunshine and strength"—not with an obvious display of dramatics but with an inner power of triumph expressed in every note of its being!

Meanwhile his music had traveled across the Atlantic, and in the autumn of 1913, Carl Stoeckel, a wealthy American, invited him to write a special work for the Litchfield County Choral Union and to go to America to conduct it in the following spring. Whereas Sibelius had hesitated about crossing the ocean, this congenial invitation won the day and he set about at once on the commissioned work. The result was the sparkling tone poem, finally called *The Oceanides*.

On May 16, 1914, Sibelius left for America; and the trip across the Atlantic—which had seemed such an undertaking in his imagination—proved a marvelous experience. In fact, the whole venture turned out to be an exciting affair. He was met at the boat by newspapermen and nameless admirers, as well as his host, Mr. Stoeckel; he was put up at a splendid hotel in New York City where he might rest before his journey to the Stoeckel home at Norfolk, Connecticut; and before he could catch his breath, Mr. Stoeckel announced to him, "Yale University plans to confer the degree of Doctor of Music on you at commencement time!"

And then on the following day they went out to the Stoeckel estate where Sibelius was entranced with the country and quite overcome with admiration for the orchestra that had been provided for the festival. He felt completely at home and tremendously stimulated.

One whole day of the three-day festival was devoted to his music: *Finlandia, Pahjola's Daughter*, the *King Christian* suite and the new work, *The Oceanides*. The concert proved a complete triumph for Sibelius: critics and public both agreed that they had heard the music of a genius. Sibelius, in turn, was vastly impressed with the excellence of the rest of the festival.

Then while waiting for the Yale event, the Stoeckels saw to it that Sibelius visited other parts of America, including Boston and Niagara Falls. It was all like a fairy tale to him, topped off with the dramatic ceremony at Yale University.

He left America with real regret, promising to return the following year, but while he was on the ocean, news came to the ship of the murder in Sarajevo that was to set aflame the First World War.

Happy to be home in Finland, despite his glorious trip to the New World, his head was abuzz with new plans—then—came the Declaration of War! It wasn't possible! Surely nations were now too civilized to fight one another!

But there was a war, and it lasted a long time—bringing misery to a great many countries, and hindering Sibelius tremendously in his work. War conditions cut off the income from his German publishers; and this worry, coupled with great anxiety for his country and family, made composing difficult. Nevertheless, he finished his fifth symphony and conducted its first performance himself on his fiftieth birthday.

Great trials assailed his country, ending with the coming of the Russian revolutionists. Sibelius, meanwhile, worked away on his sixth symphony, but the day came when, partly to protect himself and his family, he was forbidden to leave his home at Järvenpää. Then a detachment of Red Guards came to search his house.

Sibelius, fully aware that they knew neither him nor his music, was desperately concerned over his family's safety. He must carry on as though not disturbed by their intrusion; and seating himself at the piano, he played to quiet the fears of his children. Fortunately, his music had a soothing effect on the Red Guards, for one of them remarked to a faithful Sibelius servant: "It must be very pleasant to work in a house where you hear such lovely music."

But finally after another such visit by Russian Guards and great bloodshed in the surrounding country, Sibelius was persuaded to take his family into Helsingfors for the duration of the war. But he would not let the upheaval stop his composing! And we can hear in his sixth symphony the crescendo and thunder of guns, just as he did while he was composing it.

At length came release—another spring—new life. With the war over, Sibelius set about planning three symphonies: the revision of the fifth, work on the sixth and seventh. The final version of his fifth symphony was completed in the fall of 1919, but the other two took a much longer time.

Meanwhile two more *Kalevala* works developed: *Tapiola* and *Väinö's Song* And then, in 1925, came a wonderful celebration for his sixtieth birthday. Finland, free from war, could now really honor her greatest son. The State awarded him the largest pension ever given a private citizen; and orchestras all over the world performed his music.

Freed from financial worries, Sibelius could now live in his beloved Järvenpää, ignore offers from the outside world that might interfere with his composing, and work to his heart's content.

Still another war was destined to interfere with Sibelius in his northern retreat. In the fall of 1939, once again the world gone mad, began to fight—with first one country and then another being swallowed up into a great caldron—but somehow, Sibelius, in his music, gives great hope to a struggling world; for strength, individuality, integrity and courage—greatly needed—are his!

SCRIABIN

Courtesy of "Musical Courier"

ALEXANDER NIKOLAIEVITCH SCRIABIN

Mystic Composer

BORN 1872—DIED 1915

Moscow—the most hospitable city in the world—thus Raissa Soudarskaya, a noted pianist, describes the city in which her countryman and friend, Alexander Nikolaievitch Scriabin, was born on January 6, 1872. The circumstances of his birth bear out this description. His father, Nicholas Alexandrovitch Scriabin, a young law student, had married Liubov Petrovna Shchetinina, favorite pupil of the piano teacher, Theodor Leschetizky. Though he struggled manfully to provide a home for his bride, Nicholas Scriabin found it impossible. Consequently, little Alexander came into the world at the home of his grandfather, Colonel Alexander Scriabin.

Liubov Shchetinina Scriabin, falling ill within a year after her son's birth, died the following April. The grief-stricken young father went back to his studies, leaving his child with his parents. Since Colonel Scriabin died in 1879, Alexander grew up in the care of his grandmother and his aunt, Liubov Alexandrovna, who became a "second" mother to him.

Alexander, a delicate child from birth, and growing up without playmates, missed the benefits of the rough-and-tumble experience that most children enjoy. His aunt and grandmother worshiped him, and could deny him nothing.

"Isn't he adorable," one would ask the other.

He was not permitted to go on the street alone until he was well over fourteen. He was, in fact, so over-sheltered that when it came time for him to go out into the world he was frightened.

111

Meanwhile he lived a fairy-tale life under his aunt's guidance. At five he began to learn his alphabet, and by slow stages he managed to read and write by the time he was seven. But a far greater interest at the time, were the regular visits to the opera with Aunt Liubov. Sitting in the Scriabin box at the Grand Theater, little Alexander's eyes would dance with excitement as the opera stories unfolded there on the stage.

Home he would go, his mind aflame with what he had seen and heard. Climbing in and out of chairs, he would repeat the performance, in his own way, to Aunt Liubov's great delight.

A little later he wrote tragic plays in which the characters, snuffed out one by one, were all murdered at the finish.

Before he was five years old Alexander showed a natural talent for music. One day, to his aunt's amazement, after returning from the railway station where they had gone to say good-by to an uncle, Alexander sat down at the piano and played a tune that the military band had played at the station.

Now Liubov Alexandrovna understood why her nephew would lie for hours at a time, flat on his back, underneath her piano while she played. Now she understood why he bade the piano good night as though it were a living creature. Perhaps he would be a great pianist!

She must give him music lessons.

Alas, her discipline was no better at music than at reading and writing. Alexander went his merry way—improvising—finally producing an opera of a sort when he was eight.

And this happy-go-lucky way of learning went on until, at ten, Alexander, or Sasha, as he was called, entered the Second Moscow Cadet Corps. In this choice of training he followed the path of his countrymen, Modest Mussorgsky and Nikolai Rimsky-Korsakov. Military discipline proved only slightly more strict than that to which he had been accustomed under Aunt Liubov; for he lived in the home of an uncle, who was an officer in the corps. Straight-off, he also became a favorite with the director's daughter and often he played duets with her while his classmates went drilling-away at target-practice. Despite all this, Sasha was popular with his comrades, and, in general a good student.

112

In the summer of 1883 he began to take regular piano lessons from G. E. Konius, a young teacher at the Moscow Conservatory. During this period his kinship with Chopin emerged. Poetry in music—as revealed through the piano —this was born in Scriabin as it had been in Chopin; and his first real composition, A Canon in D minor and a Nocturne in A flat, dating, as far as can be determined, from the spring of 1884, illustrated this unconscious kinship.

That spring Sasha fell seriously ill, but though as a result, he became more delicate in health and nature than ever, he came out at the head of his class the following year. He had now definitely decided to be a musician; but first of all, he must finish the prescribed study at the Cadet School.

Once he had decided to become a musician, he set about preparing to enter the Moscow Conservatory. With this in mind, he began to study the piano with N. S. Zverev—a Conservatory teacher of unusual ability—who, at the time, numbered among his pupils the future composer and pianist, Sergei Rachmaninov.

Sasha made great strides with his new teacher and soon became a favorite pupil, playing "magnificently" at Zverev's Sunday-night recitals. After watching his guests enjoy Sasha's playing of music by Schumann, Liszt, and other composers, Zverev would proudly announce, "Now 'Scriabushka' will play one of his own compositions. This may have been his waltz in D flat—once more a direct descendant of Chopin, for it was during this period that he slept, ate and thought *Chopin*. According to his friend Madame Soudarskaya, he often went to sleep at night, with pages of Chopin's music tucked under his pillow!

After a few preliminary lessons in musical theory from Taneiev, young Scriabin, in 1888, at sixteen, entered the Moscow Conservatory. He studied counterpoint with Taneiev, fugue and composition with Arensky and piano with Vassily Safonov who later went to America where he became conductor of the New York Philharmonic Society.

Safonov was enchanted with Sasha's piano playing, particularly his pedaling. Once when Scriabin was playing, Safonov said to the class, "Watch his feet, not his hands." And the highest praise a pupil could hope for—was to be told that he had "Sasha-like pedaling."

113

Unaccustomed to rivalry, Scriabin became distressed when the playing of a classmate showed greater technical brilliance than his. He must change that at once! And he began to practice with such intensity that for a time he lost the use of his right hand. Nothing daunted, he wrote music for *one* hand, including his *Prelude and Nocturne* for the left hand only.

Though he had written music enough to merit a composition diploma, he annoyed Arensky so thoroughly by going off on "tangents"—neglecting to confine himself to assignments—that the two came to the parting of the ways before Sasha had taken his final examinations.

Soon after leaving the Conservatory, some of his music—including two of his popular preludes—was printed by the publisher, Jurgenson. This did not put him in the top rank of composers, however, for he was thought of, chiefly, as a brilliant pianist.

The spring of 1894, Scriabin had the good fortune to attract the attention of Belaiev, who had become a kind of fairy-godfather to Russian musicians. Seeing some of Scriabin's piano pieces, Belaiev was vastly impressed with them; and when he had heard the Chopinesque young Russian *play* at his St. Petersburg recital that spring, he was enchanted. *He* must publish Scriabin's music.

Accordingly, generous arrangements were made at once with the approval of Sasha's grandmother and Aunt Liubov. Belaiev remained Scriabin's publisher until 1908, and took particular delight in supervising his concert tours. Not content to make the arrangements, Belaiev, on the first concert trip in 1895, always sat on the platform with his protégé. Going first to Heidelberg, Dresden and Berlin, they stayed for a time, in the spring, near Lucerne where Scriabin composed several of his preludes. From there they went southward to Italy; then home until the next season, when Scriabin played in Paris, Berlin, Amsterdam and Brussels.

Paris found Scriabin exceptionally interesting as a philosophical composer-pianist; while he, in turn, felt spiritually at home there. The feather-like quality of his music and playing, enchanting the French audiences, they claimed him as their own—the "Russian Chopin."

That fall, Scriabin became engaged to a brilliant young pianist, Vera Ivanovna Isakovitch, a student at the Moscow Conservatory. Having met her in 1893, at a memorial concert for Nicholas Rubinstein, he had been attracted by her piano playing, thinking to himself, "At last, here is a woman pianist to whom I can listen with pleasure."

Married in the spring of 1897, they went to the Crimea for their honeymoon where Scriabin finished his Second Sonata and wrote his only Piano Concerto. In October he played in the first performance of the Concerto under Safonov at Odessa, and immediately afterward went to Paris with his young wife.

While in Paris, a mysterious letter arrived from the critic, Vladmir Stassov, announcing that Scriabin had been awarded a prize of one thousand rubles by an unknown person—one who had been giving money to Russian composers, of his choosing, each Glinka's day—thus named to commemorate the first production date of Glinka's operas, *Russlan and Ludmilla* and *Life For the Tsar*. These awards came to Scriabin for several years. Not until Belaiev died in 1904 was the secret revealed: Belaiev had been the silent benefactor as well as an open donor of grand piano, scores and other gifts.

Meanwhile Scriabin and Vera Ivanovna, having given a joint recital of his compositions in Paris, returned to Moscow and settled at Maidanovo, for the summer. There a daughter, named Rimma, was born to them, and there Scriabin composed his Third Sonata.

Returning to Moscow, Scriabin found that his income—sufficient for himself—was inadequate for the support of a wife and baby. Consequently, when Safonov, on the death of Vera Ivanovna's teacher, P. Y. Schloezer, offered him the piano professorship at the Conservatory, he gladly accepted.

Unlike Rimsky-Korsakov, Scriabin was no teacher. Though he fired a few pupils with his own emotional excitement, he was too vague, in thought and in action, to transmit his knowledge to others. "The feeling of art—above all!" he would demand of his pupils. Since one cannot learn the "feeling of art" by command, the results were seldom remarkable.

His own nervous excitement grew in leaps and bounds. At home, where two more daughters and a son were born, Vera Ivanovna tried her utmost to make

115

life comfortable for her husband. Scarcely ever playing the piano herself, she gave him a room, removed from the children, so that he might not be disturbed.

Becoming possessed with the dream of writing a "large" work, the idea of developing art as a religion grew in his mind; in the spring of 1899, Safonov conducted his first orchestral work, Rêverie; and Scriabin then wrote his First Symphony in E minor, which was given its first performance in the spring of 1901, with only moderate success. Scriabin became all the more determined to achieve something "big"!

His mind turned more and more to philosophy. He became a close friend of the mystic philosopher, Prince Trubetskoy, who, in turn, greatly admired Scriabin's music. He dipped into Goethe's *Faust*; became interested in Wagner's ideas of art, life and music; turned to Nietzsche from Wagner, and became convinced that his music would revolutionize the world. He began to express these ideas in a philosophical opera, never finished, while at the same time he worked on his second symphony. Again, this was given its first performance under Safonov, who continued to call Scriabin "a great composer."

The fall of 1902, Scriabin met a young woman whose friendship changed the course of his life. Her name was Tatiana Feodorovna Schloezer. Having heard Scriabin's Third Sonata at a recital the year before at Piatigorsk, in the Caucasus, she had dedicated her piano playing to his music from that moment. She had now come to Moscow to study composition, never dreaming that she might study with her idol. After meeting him at the home of her brother, and sitting entranced at *his* piano playing, she had mustered enough courage to show him some of her own compositions. Scriabin *offered* to teach her! Under the influence of his personality, she gave up thoughts of composing herself, but continued to study with Scriabin in order to understand his music better.

The following spring, Scriabin having decided to devote his time to composition, resigned from the Moscow Conservatory. He had decided to go to Switzerland to live, but he must, first, earn some extra money. Accordingly, burying himself in the country, and, working at fever-pitch, he composed his Fourth Sonata and thirty-five shorter piano pieces.

He could not, however, make enough to support his family. Then at the end of the year, with Belaiev's death, his mysterious allowance stopped. At the right moment, another friend, this time a former pupil, M. K. Morogova, came forward with a promise of an annual sum. Money matters settled, the Scriabins went in the spring of 1904 to Switzerland, where they settled at Vêsenaz on Lake Geneva. Tatiana Schloezer followed, stopping at Belle-Rive not far from Vêsenaz.

Switzerland fascinated Scriabin. There he could be himself and work out his ideas of a new world. Finding the people receptive, he even preached to them from a boat, "like Christ." His third symphony, the *Divine Poem*, just finished, would transform the world! Convinced of his mission, after coaching Vera Ivanovna in the playing of all his compositions in order that she might lead an independent life, he announced that he was going to leave her—as "a sacrifice to art." Thus, with the *Divine Poem* copied out and ready for performance, he left for Paris.

Artur Nikisch conducted the first performance of the *Divine Poem* in Paris on May 29, 1905. The music combined with Tatiana Schloezer's program, written to describe Scriabin's attempt at uniting music with philosophy—attracted wide attention. Scriabin then having become interested in Madame Blavatsky's theosophy, went to Italy the following spring. There in the company of his art-companion, Tatiana Schloezer, he began work on his second orchestral composition, *Poem of Ecstasy.* Meanwhile Vera Ivanovna, now a teacher at the Moscow Conservatory, gave all-Scriabin concerts in various cities.

Scriabin then went through a difficult period. Having lost favor with his publishers, after Belaiev's death, he turned, unsuccessfully, in various directions to find a new publisher. Settled now at Geneva, he gave a recital of his music, and worked at the *Poem of Ecstasy.*

When his financial situation was desperate, he learned about Modest Altschuler's Russian concerts in New York City. He would write to him at once! Altschuler not only asked him to send his scores but invited him to America to make a personal appearance in his own concerto. Accordingly, in the fall of 1906, after giving two recitals in Brussels, Scriabin set out for

117

America. Arrived there, he attended two of Altschuler's concerts, which included his First Symphony and the *Divine Poem*, at Carnegie Hall.

Leaving America, he arrived in Paris in time for Sergei Diaghilev's historic Russian concerts. Josef Hofmann, who greatly admired Scriabin's music, played his Concerto at one concert, and Nikisch conducted his Second Symphony at another.

Meanwhile Scriabin took advantage of the presence of so many Russian composers in Paris to introduce to them bits of his *Poem of Ecstasy*. He also outlined the plan of his projected work—*Mystery*. Though Rimsky-Korsakov, among those present, did not respond to Scriabin's music, he was interested in his theories about color in relation to music, and he became enough reconciled to the mystic composer to agree with the other members of the Belaiev board of directors to publish his *Poem of Ecstasy*, when finished.

Thus encouraged, Scriabin and Tatiana set out for Switzerland, where with desperate effort, the score of *Poem of Ecstasy* was finished in January 1908. While in Switzerland Scriabin also composed some smaller pieces, gave recitals and decided to publish his own music. He would let Belaiev's firm have his large works, but he would publish his piano works himself! Little did he know the complications involved in such a procedure: at the end of two years he had received a few coins for his trouble!

The spring of 1908, fate again stepped into the picture when Sergei Kussevitsky, who had just made his debut in Berlin, paid a visit to Scriabin. Kussevitsky, with money at his disposal, wanted to manage concerts in Russia and found a Russian publishing house. He needed a star-composer—Scriabin needed a backer! They liked each other, the result being that Kussevitsky agreed to take all money worries from Scriabin while he finished his monumental *Mystery*. Meanwhile, Scriabin turning over small pieces to Kussevitsky would act as advisor to the publishing venture.

Before starting this colossal undertaking, Scriabin went to Brussels where he buried himself in theosophy, and devised a new system of language for his *Mystery*. In the midst of these dallyings, he was called to Berlin by Kussevitsky.

Soon afterward he attended an all-Scriabin concert in Moscow. His music now aroused tremendous interest, particularly among musicians. The concert, unusually successful, was repeated as a benefit performance. With these performances of the *Divine Poem* and *Poem of Ectasy*, "Scriabinism" was born in Russia!

After giving several recitals in Moscow, Scriabin returned to Brussels, where again finding the atmosphere congenial, he remained most of the year 1909. And he began another large orchestral work, *Prometheus: A Poem of Fire* in which he included a wordless chorus and directions for a color organ accompaniment.

The beginning of 1910, he returned to Moscow for good. Shortly afterward Scriabin and Tatiana went with Kussevitsky on the first of his Volga Tours, after which, settling in the country for the summer, Scriabin finished *Prometheus*. Given its first performance under Kussevitsky—with Scriabin playing the piano part, but with the color feature eliminated—*Prometheus* failed to please its first audience.

Soon after this concert, Kussevitsky and Scriabin came to the parting of the ways, though Kussevitsky continued to play and publish Scriabin's music.

Scriabin, after another summer of work in the country, went on an extensive tour. During the winter he was reinstated, on generous terms, with his first publishing firm, Jurgenson's; the following summer he spent in Switzerland; then came more concerts, then—home to Moscow. Concerts again occupied his time but the season was made memorable by a visit to England that spring. Scriabin loved England and he vowed that he would return the next year.

Meanwhile his mind was astir with his *Mystery*. Convinced that the world must die and be reborn, his composition was planned to be performed by one and all as a bridge into a new existence. Since the world was not ready for this "purification," he wrote out the text of what he called the *Preliminary Action* as a rehearsal for the *Mystery*.

Though, as he told his friends, the music was all in his head, destiny interrupted the great venture. Shortly after a successful concert in the spring

119

of 1915, Scriabin fell ill with—what seemed to be—a boil on his lip. Fever and complications developed, and he died on the morning of April 27, 1915.

Scriabin's music, chiefly through its individual treatment of harmonies, gives the impression of soaring skyward; and his mystical poetical nature reveals itself most poignantly in music for the piano—preludes and sonatas.

VAUGHAN WILLIAMS

RALPH VAUGHAN WILLIAMS

England—City and Countryside

BORN 1872

Ralph Vaughan Williams, destined to bring a genuine English spirit to the world of music, was born on October 12, 1872, at Down Ampney, Gloucestershire, England. Edward Elgar was a boy of fifteen, and Frederick Delius was ten.

When his father, who was a clergyman, saw that his young son showed an interest in music, he planned his education accordingly. Musician or banker, Ralph must be trained to earn his living! With this in mind, the elder Vaughan Williams sent his son after three years of general education at Charter House School, London, to the Royal College of Music for two years. Following that, young Vaughan Williams went to Trinity College, Cambridge, where he received the degree of Bachelor of Music, after which he studied still another year at the Royal College of Music.

Though from the beginning his interest was in composing—with his father's admonition about earning a living in mind—he studied both piano and organ. And on leaving the Royal College of Music, he became organist at South Lambeth Church in London. In the winter of 1907-08 he studied for a time with Max Bruch at the Akademie der Künste in Berlin. And the following year he spent a few months in Paris studying under Maurice Ravel who was three years younger than he, but musically more advanced.

Though subjected to various influences, he retained his individuality. True, he had written no music of which he was proud, but he was on the way, and soon after taking his doctor's degree in music at Cambridge in 1901, he found the key to his future—the English folk-song.

Whereas countries like Russia, Bohemia and Hungary had been delving into their folklore for sometime, England was only just becoming aware of her own folk-song heritage. And in 1904 Vaughan Williams joined the Folk-Song Society, one of the pioneer groups in searching out English folk-tunes.

As a result of this, he wrote his three *Norfolk Rhapsodies* for orchestra, based directly on folk-tunes. But it was not long before he realized that this was not to be *his* way of using his country's folk material. He would express an Englishness, for that was his nature, but not in this direct transplanting-of-tunes into his own music. And his two choral works based on poems by Walt Whitman illustrate this new feeling: *Toward The Unknown Region* was given at the Leeds Festival in 1907 and *A Sea Symphony* appeared at the same festival in 1910.

Other compositions of this period include his folk-opera, *Hugh the Drover*, an overture to Aristophanes' *Wasps* and his Fantasia on the Theme by Tallis for strings. The Fantasia based on music of Thomas Tallis, an early church composer, has become one of his most popular works.

Then in 1914 Vaughan Williams completed a work that placed him among leading composers of his day. This was *A London Symphony* which paints in music the sights, sounds and feeling of London, not by realistic reproduction but by tonal suggestion. During the course of this symphony popular tunes walk into the music, unadorned, but they belong there as part of the impression. In this work Vaughan Williams came into his own!

Once again the War interrupted an artist's creative life. Though Vaughan Williams was over forty years old, he enlisted and served, first as a stretcher-bearer, and later, as an officer in the artillery in France.

Home from the war, he joined the faculty of the Royal College of Music and became conductor of the London Bach Choir.

During the following decade he occupied himself, not so much with the folk background of his country as, with the music of the early English composers, with madrigals, and with early church music. To this period belongs his cantata, *The Shepherds of the Delectable Mountains*, the ballet, *Old King*

Cole, the violin and orchestra work, *The Lark Ascending,* the beautiful suite for viola, orchestra and voices, *Flos campi,* a mass, an oratorio, a violin concerto and the famous *A Pastoral Symphony.* This symphony evokes warm memories of the countryside, of nature's magical change of seasons; and promises peace and calm to the listener.

Vaughan Williams, continuing to develop as a composer, now began to write a different kind of music, more strident, more direct. Characteristic of this style are his later works, *Riders To The Sea,* a musical setting to Synge's play, and his Symphony No. 4 in F minor. Also, a delicious humor often appeared in his music, such as in the opera, *Sir John in Love,* and the comic-opera, *The Poisoned Kiss.*

In 1935, through his receiving the Order of Merit, Vaughan Williams was officially admitted to the company of England's Great Ones. But the writing of his "London" and "Pastoral" symphonies, if nothing else, had already placed him there—Vaughan Williams—England!

SCHOENBERG

Courtesy of "Musical Courier"

ARNOLD SCHOENBERG

Stenciler of Tone Patterns

BORN 1874

Arnold Schoenberg—destined to become the most controversial figure in modern music—was born in Vienna on September 13, 1874. Spiritual son of Wagner, Brahms and Richard Strauss, some inner urge was to force him to break the known framework of music and to invent new patterns of his own.

While a pupil at the Realschule, he learned to play the violin and later taught himself to play the violoncello, but he never "took music lessons" as most boys and girls do today. At the same time, unlike many boys and girls he practiced without being urged, for he wanted desperately to learn.

And soon he was not only playing in a small amateur group of musicians but he was writing music for them to play!

When Arnold was sixteen years old, his father who was a merchant, died; and Arnold found himself face to face with earning his own living. At the same time he continued to study music by himself—to devour scores of the masters—and to make experiments in composition.

By the time he was twenty, he had written a fair amount of music. And one day, a friend suggested that he show some of it to a noted composer and conductor by the name of Alexander von Zemlinsky. Zemlinsky was sufficiently impressed to encourage young Schoenberg, and, at the same time, offered to teach him counterpoint. This instruction, lasting only a few months was all Schoenberg ever had.

He and Zemlinsky, however, became good friends. Both were members

of an orchestral society, Polyhymnia, in which Schoenberg played the violoncello and Zemlinsky conducted. Then at twenty-three, Schoenberg made a
piano arrangement of Zemlinsky's opera, *Sarema;* and shortly afterward he
wrote a string quartet—his first composition to be publicly performed. It is
interesting to observe that though Schoenberg's music became more and more
"modern" it always kept roots in these chamber music days.

Meanwhile Schoenberg often met with a group of young musicians at a
café where their informal meetings took on the character of a seminar—with
Wagner's score of *Tristan* the teacher, or at any rate, the center of discussion.
And Schoenberg's early songs—first sung in public in 1900 by Eduard
Gärtener—bear kinship to these Wagner-café days. Definitely individual in
style and employing an unfamiliar range and combination of sounds, they
met with some opposition which steadily grew with each new Schoenberg
composition.

In 1899 he wrote his first major composition—*Verklärte Nacht,* or, *The
Night Transfigured*—a sextet for strings. It is based on a poem by Richard
Dehmel and clearly expresses in music the power of love and forgiveness,
against a background of crystal moonlight.

During the following year Schoenberg began work on his extraordinary
cantata, the *Gurre-Lieder,* written for five solo singers, three four-part male
choruses, an eight-part chorus of mixed voices and a narrator. To the amazement of his friends, he ordered special-size paper with sixty-five staves printed
for the scoring of his new work. But he firmly insisted that this breaking the
bounds of normal composition, was not a matter of bravado or showmanship
but in his words—"following an inner compulsion that is stronger than education, and obeying a law that is natural to me, and therefore stronger than
my artistic training!"

By 1901 *Gurre-Lieder* had been completely sketched out but Schoenberg
had to lay the orchestrating aside in order to work on light opera scores to
make a living. Just having married Mathilde von Zemlinsky, his friend's
sister, he was faced with new responsibilities. During the same year he moved
to Berlin where for a time he conducted at Ernst von Wolzogen's Buntes
Theater, an artistic cabaret. But soon, having attracted the attention of

Richard Strauss, he was awarded the Liszt Scholarship and appointed teacher at the Stern Conservatory in Berlin.

In 1903 he returned to Vienna where he began to teach harmony and composition at the Schwarzwald School. His first pupils included Alban Berg, Egon Wellesz, Anton von Webern and Irwin Stein, all of whom later did credit to their teacher. Without exception, his pupils sang his praises as a teacher; for unlike many composers who resent giving their time to teaching, Schoenberg made a creative thing of teaching and thus both he and pupils benefited.

Meanwhile his chamber music was being played by various organizations including the Rose Quartet. And it was at a rehearsal of this group that Schoenberg met Gustav Mahler, who was genuinely interested in his music, though not in complete agreement with his "revolutionary" ideas.

In 1904 Schoenberg helped organize the Vereinigung Schaffender Tokünstler for the promotion of a free art. And at the beginning of the New Year he conducted his symphonic poem, *Pelleas and Melisande*, composed while he was in Berlin, at one of the Society's concerts. The strangeness of the music brought a storm of protest down upon his head, but also attracted new followers.

Then in order to express still further an inner urge, Schoenberg, for a time, turned to painting. And in 1910 he held an exhibit of these paintings-from-necessity in Vienna. At about this time he was appointed teacher of composition at the Imperial Academy of Music; he gave many lectures; and as he continued to compose, each new composition grew further afield from the accepted tonality or pattern in music.

In addition, he completed his important *Harmonielehre,* or *Manual of Harmony* in 1911, and dedicated it to the memory of Gustav Mahler who had just died. The preface of the book begins—"This book I have learnt from my pupils"—an attitude which somewhat explains Schoenberg's talent for teaching.

The following year, audiences became more and most hostile at performances of his work which included *Five Pieces for Orchestra* and his song-cycle, *Pierrot Lunaire,* also known as "Three Times Seven Songs."

Then on February 23, 1913, his colossal work, *Gurre-Lieder*, finished in 1911, was given in Vienna under Franz Schreker with nearly four hundred performers. This performance was immensely successful, but later audiences have had little opportunity to hear it—although the very beautiful *Wood Dove's Song* is sometimes given by itself.

To his composing, teaching and lecturing, Schoenberg had now added conducting; and Amsterdam, St. Petersburg and London were among the cities that he visited. Then in 1914 the First World War interrupted the course of his life, just as it had that of Elgar, Delius, Sibelius and many thousands of others.

After several periods of military service, he settled down at Mödling, near Vienna, where he held his famous seminar for Composition. Many new pupils joined him there and took part in a Society for Private Musical Performances which Schoenberg organized for the purpose of giving concerts of modern music.

In 1920 after attending a Mahler Festival held at Amsterdam, Schoenberg gave a course of lectures there. Returning to Mödling, he continued with his teaching and modern-concert-giving. Then in 1924 Vienna paid tribute to Schoenberg's fiftieth birthday: a dedicatory volume was issued by his friends and pupils; a concert was held in the Town Hall; and Universal Edition publishers opened—free of charge for the use of students—the Arnold Schoenberg Library of Modern Music. On the same day his Quintet for Flute, Oboe, Clarinet, Bassoon and Horn—using the twelve-tone principle—was given its first performance in Vienna.

Surely a wonderful birthday despite the opposition to his music from the strictly conservative ones!

In the following year he was appointed professor of a master-class at the Prussian Academy of Arts in Berlin. This was a position previously held by the composer and pianist, Ferruccio Busoni. And Schoenberg remained there until 1933 when—once again the world being in the midst of a great turmoil—he was dismissed by the German Ministry of Education.

Leaving Europe by way of Paris, he went to America where he taught at the Malkin Conservatory in Boston. Meanwhile many concerts were given to celebrate his arrival in the United States including one by the New York League of Composers and one by the Library of Congress.

He was appointed professor of music at the University of California in 1935, and he accepted a similar position at the University of Southern California the following year.

Arnold Schoenberg abandoned key-relationships—this, in part—states his story. Only one composition since his F sharp minor string quartet in 1907 bears a key signature, or in other words, an indication of its tonality. But this does not mean that his music runs wild without form or unity. In what we know as "tonal" music—the music to which our ears have been accustomed—there is always a root, or fundamental tone to which all parts of a composition refer; whereas in—what Schoenberg chooses to call—"pantonal" music there are patterns of tones regardless of their relationship to one another: parts, patterns or "motives" of musical ideas are added together to make a whole.

And though Schoenberg's "pantonal" music sounds strange to our key-tuned ears, it does open new musical worlds!

RAVEL

MAURICE RAVEL

Grill-work that Dances

BORN 1875—DIED 1937

Maurice Joseph Ravel, known to the world as Maurice Ravel, was born on March 7, 1875, less than a year after the birth of Arnold Schoenberg, at Ciboure, a seascoast-French-Basque town near Saint-Jean-de-Luz, just across the border from Spain. His mother was of Basque descent and his father, French-Swiss. Thus he was kin—both by birthplace and parentage —to those colorful Basque people, half-French and half-Spanish, who dwell in the Pyrenees.

When Maurice was very young his parents moved to Paris, and there he received his education. Curiously enough, unlike the parents of Delius, Dvořák, and Humperdinck, Maurice's father, an engineer and music-lover, encouraged his son to study music.

He began to take piano lessons from Henri Ghis when he was twelve years old; while at the same time he took up the study of harmony with Charles René, who immediately recognized an individual quality in his young pupil.

In 1889, Maurice was permitted to enter Anthione's Preparatory Piano Class at the Paris Conservatoire where he progressed sufficiently well to be admitted, in 1891, to Charles de Bériot's class. There he made the acquaintance of a fellow-pupil Ricardo Viñes, who became a noted pianist, famous particularly for his playing of Ravel's music.

Meanwhile young Ravel studied harmony at the Conservatoire with Émile Pessard. But while he was learning the strict rules of composition at the

Conservatoire, he was eagerly taking part in the revolt against tradition, then sweeping Paris by storm. At times he shocked his professor with the strangeness of his harmony exercises; and on many occasions, he entertained his classmates, while waiting for Professor Pessard's arrival, by playing some of the "new" music he had heard outside the Conservatoire. This was likely to be bits of Erik Satie's music—the titles of which were enough to startle the tardy professor—as for instance, *Genuine lazy preludes for a dog,* or *Disagreeable glimpses.*

Ravel had now begun to compose pieces of his own, and though not so picturesque in title, they were, nevertheless, highly individual in style. *Menuet antique* for piano was composed in 1895, followed by the *Sites Auriculaires* for two pianos which include the *Habanera* later used in his *Rapsodie Espagnole.* And it was in 1898 that he made his debut as a composer with the *Sites Auriculaires* performed at a Société Nationale de Musique concert. The following year the same society gave his *Schéhérazade* overture and the delicate *Pavana pour une Infante defunte* in its original piano version.

Meanwhile he began to study counterpoint from André Gédalge and composition from Gabriel Fauré. Gédalge considered him a brilliant student and Fauré—a man free from hide-bound academic traditions—recognizing Ravel's individual tendencies, encouraged their spontaneous development with rare balance of judgment.

From 1901 to 1905 Ravel battled unsuccessfully for the highly coveted Prix de Rome. Although he composed unusually brilliant works during that period—*Jeux d'Eaux* for piano, the String Quartet in F, and a song-cycle, *Schéhérazade*—this academic honor was denied him. In 1921 he was awarded the second prize for his cantata, *Myrrha;* in 1902 and 1903 he again entered the contest, but in 1905 he did not even pass the preliminary test. This brought down a storm of protest from the French musical public, resulting in the change of directorship of the Conservatoire.

Fortunately, these repeated disappointments did not hinder Ravel's composing. In 1905 he finished his jewel-like Sonatine for piano and composed the *Miroirs,* a collection of piano pieces bearing kinship to Debussy, but more direct and clean-cut in outline. Then came the *Histoires Naturelles*, a collection of dryly humorous declamations for voice and piano and as a natural outgrowth of this style—*L'Heure Espagnole*, a comic-opera in one act. Meanwhile he had found time to write the subtly persuasive piece of chamber music, *Introduction and Allegro*, for harp, string quartet, flute and clarinet.

The following year he composed his very moving *Rapsodie Espagnole* or *Spanish Rhapsody*. Slight changes of rhythm and careful blending of instruments in this provocative, orchestral work revealed Ravel's truly remarkable mastery of the orchestra.

In 1908 he composed three pieces for the piano under the title *Gaspard de la Nuit*—these also revealing a master's touch. In them new possibilities were evoked from the piano, and one pianist remarked that it took exactly twenty-seven different methods of touch to interpret *Le Gibet*—one of the three pieces—properly!

Just when Ravel might have been accused of over-sophistication, he up and wrote the charming *Mother Goose* set of duets for two young friends of his! In that form it was given its first performance at the Salle Gaveau, Paris, April 20, 1910, by Christane Verger, six years old and Germaine Duramy who was ten. Later it was orchestrated for ballet and revised for concert performances. In this arrangement the five numbers include: "Pavane of the Sleeping Beauty," "Hop-o'-My-Thumb," "Laideronette, Empress of the Pogodes," "Beauty and the Beast" and "The Fairy Garden."

Then Ravel attracted the attention of that master-showman Sergei Diaghilev who commissioned him to write the ballet *Daphnis and Chloë*. Given its first production by the Ballet Russe at the Châtelet, Paris, June 8, 1912 with Nijinsky and Karsavina in the leading rôles, it met with sensational success and since that time, in the form of two orchestral suites, it is frequently played by orchestras all over the world.

Fastidious by nature, and realizing that in orchestration he could go no further than in *Daphnis and Chloë* without becoming over-elaborate, Ravel wrote in a much simpler style in his next composition, *Trois Poèms de Mallarmé* for voice, piano, two flutes and two clarinets. This characteristic

139

continued in his Piano Trio and became marked in *Le Tombeau de Couperin* written for piano and later arranged, in part, for orchestra.

Then for two years Ravel served as an ambulance driver in the First World War, until broken in health, he was demobilized in 1917. After a rest cure, he wrote his orchestral piece *La Valse* which was given its first performance at Paris, December 12, 1920. On the score is the following description: "whirling clouds give glimpses, through rifts, of couples waltzing. The clouds scatter, little by little. One sees an immense hall, peopled with a twirling crowd. The scene is gradually illuminated. The light of the chandeliers bursts forth, fortissimo. An imperial court about 1855." This is exactly what the music miraculously suggests; but the lovely waltz rhythm becomes distorted, menacing and wild, and carries with it some of the bitterness growing out of the experiences in a war that was supposed to have saved democracy.

The sonata for violin and violoncello came next, followed by his opera-ballet *L'Enfant et les Sortilèges*, first produced at Monte Carlo in 1925.

Though the composer of all this genuinely individual music, Ravel held aloof from the world, and in truth, the world paid no remarkable heed of him. But in 1928 he was commissioned to write a ballet for Ida Rubinstein, the result of which made his name as famous as the composer of the latest popular dance tune. This was *Bolero,* which, when given its first performance by Ida Rubinstein at the Paris Opèra in November 1928, nearly caused a riot. Arturo Toscanini introduced it to American audiences at a New York Philharmonic concert on November 14, 1929, and within two weeks "Ravel" and "Bolero" had become practically household words!

Bolero is actually an orchestral stunt, but written with such subtle use of instrumental combinations that it transcends its own origin. One theme weaves, twists and twines itself relentlessly, without becoming monotonous over a steady rhythm that mounts and mounts in intensity, until with a slight variation of theme the piece ends in a tremendous clash of tone.

Since the war Ravel had been living in seclusion at a villa in Montfort l'Amaury, not far from Paris. But the success of *Bolero* played havoc with this way of life. He became, overnight, the most sought-after musical figure in France; and after that, often appeared in various cities as guest-conductor of his own work.

Between 1930 and 1932 he worked on two piano concertos. One was the Concerto in G major, given its first performance at Paris on January 14, 1932; and the other one, was the Concerto for the Left Hand, played for the first time by Paul Wittgenstein, for whom it was written at Paris, January 17, 1933, under Ravel's conducting.

In November 1934, he completed *Don Quichotte à Dulcinée*, consisting of three songs for baritone and orchestra. This was destined to be his last creative work, for he was stricken with a brain disorder and died, in Paris, following an operation on December 28, 1937.

Ravel—creator of controlled designs of crystal-clear music. An objective artist, never revealing his own personality, but at the same time, out of filigree melodies, creating subtle tapestries of song—graceful in movement—this is Ravel!

CARPENTER

JOHN ALDEN CARPENTER

American Impressionist

BORN 1876

Jᴏʜɴ Aʟᴅᴇɴ Cᴀʀᴘᴇɴᴛᴇʀ, whose name immediately makes us think of the Pilgrims—of John Alden, Priscilla and Miles Standish—was born on February 28, 1876, at Park Ridge, Illinois. Born in the month of heroes, and linked in name to the early Americans, he was destined to become not a general, not a governor, and not President of the United States, but one of America's most distinguished composers.

His mother, a talented amateur singer, was delighted when her son showed an early interest in music. And fortunately, it was possible for her husband, a successful business man, to provide the boy with excellent music teachers in Chicago. For a time he took piano lessons from Amy Fay who had been a pupil of Liszt at Weimar and later he studied with William Seeboeck, a former pupil of Brahms and Anton Rubinstein.

Then when he went to Harvard University to complete his general education, he continued the study of musical theory under John K. Paine. Graduated from Harvard in 1897, young Carpenter entered his father's firm—dealers in mill-railway and shipping supplies.

This might have spelled the doom of young musical dreams for one of weaker purpose, but not for John Alden Carpenter! Instead, his business career, at first, made it possible for him to pursue his music study, and later, left him free from commercial consideration when composing music.

For a short time, in 1906, he studied with Edward Elgar while both were in Rome on a visit. Then for the next four years he continued the study of musical theory under Berenhard Ziehn in Chicago.

Gradually his own composing took shape. His first significant published works were *Improving Songs for Anxious Children*, which appeared in 1907; his sonata for violin and piano was first performed in public by the Schola Cantorum Society in New York City on December 11, 1912; and in 1914, his song-cycle to poems by the Indian poet, Tagore, brought him close to the doors of fame. The titles of the songs in this cycle are *When I Bring You Colored Toys, On the Day When Death Will Knock at Thy Door, The Sleep that Flits on Baby's Eyes, I am Like a Remnant of a Cloud in Autumn, On the Seashore of Endless Worlds* and *Light my Light*.

But it took his pondering-over-the-thoughts-of-a-baby, in music, *Adventures in a Perambulator*, to bring him real renown. And this droll orchestral suite did not become popular over-night. Given its first performance by the Chicago Symphony Orchestra on March 19, 1915, it has gradually become recognized by orchestras and audiences all over the world.

Suppose we peek into what John Alden Carpenter *thinks in music*—a baby thinks about—in his *Adventures in a Perambulator:*

First of all, having had his second breakfast, the baby, who is the hero in this adventure, wonders what sort of day it is going to be. And lo! because the sun is bright and the wind is kind, an immense human being—to his eyes —his nurse, wraps him in woolens, buckles him into his carriage and off they go to the park!

What a wonderful new world! Everything is strange. The smells are different. The sounds are different. But how exciting everything is! Then a new "someone" appears—first in feeling—then in fact. He is still more immense than Nurse—and more powerful. Even Nurse becomes meek in his "blue" presence. He is the Policeman! Nurse and he talk together for a while until our hero, feeling left out of things, becomes impatient and in no uncertain terms, reminds Nurse that he is THERE. The Policeman, without batting an eye, moves away but his "feeling" remains.

Suddenly, something appears. A sound. A gay "twinkly" sound. And it comes from a box, a mountain-of-a-music-box on wheels. First a dark man

146

turns a handle that makes this lovely music, then a beautifully dressed lady takes turns at it while he rests. Just when the sound becomes so gay that our perambulator-rider is tempted to dance about with "Nurse" and his carriage, that "feeling" appears. It is the Policeman to chase the lovely sound away. He glances at Nurse for approval as he disappears. And from the distance comes the forbidden music!

Nurse and Baby push on. All of a sudden the land stops and there are little dancing waves bobbing up and down in the sun, with a white seagull floating above. It is a lake.

Surely there can be nothing more! But there is! There are dozens of a new "something"—dogs! Little ones, big ones, fuzzy ones. And they frolic and play until the whole park rings with their laughter.

They have gone! Everything is gone. What a strange world. Our wanderer feels happy and safe, when closing his eyes, he feels Nurse's firm touch on the handle of his perambulator. Just for a moment he thinks Nurse is his mother, for he is going to sleep. He is re-living the day's adventures. And he is happy—in such a strange way!

The following year, Carpenter had great fun writing his concertino for piano and orchestra. In it, the piano and orchestra, like two friends meeting after a long separation "chat" together about their experiences. His symphony, *Sermons in Stones,* was given its first performance on June 5, 1917, at the Litchfield County Choral Union Festival held at Norfolk, Connecticut; his ballet-pantomime, *The Birthday of the Infanta,* was given by the Chicago Opera Company on December 23, 1919, and his ballet, *Krazy-Kat,* based on the famous cartoon by George Herriman was given, in 1923 in Chicago. Krazy-Kat's puckish humor bubbles up in the music; and jazz fiends help bring the cartoons to life.

Then on February 19, 1926, the Metropolitan Opera Company of New York gave the first performance of Carpenter's ballet, *Skyscrapers.* In it, he gives us his impression of the modern machine age of rivets and mechanism. A series of impressions of American city life—divided between work and play—takes the place of a story. Restlessness prevails in the opening scene; then the "Skyscraper" theme appears. Men are at work, passers-by stop to watch and make remarks. Work stops and gradually a new rhythm comes into the music. A fox-trot melody gives the impression of an amusement park—Coney Island—perhaps. The sound of a brass band, and carrousel blare out as the ballet moves into the amusement center. A "Strutter's Dance" appears, then a Negro-blues scene, followed by a "Sandwich Man" section. the factory whistle calls the merry-makers back to work. Once more the "Skyscraper" swallows up the people in the music!

Though few have had an opportunity to enjoy *Skyscrapers* in ballet-form, many have heard the condensed orchestral versions.

John Alden Carpenter—impressionist painter in music, as the title for his songs to four Chinese poems, *Water Colors*, suggests; but in spite of avoiding bold, solid colors, he has written music that has strength, character, and healthy humor.

FALLA

MANUEL de FALLA

Spanish in Rhythm, Melody and Spirit

BORN 1876

Mᴀɴᴜᴇʟ Mᴀʀíᴀ ᴅᴇ Fᴀʟʟᴀ ʏ Mᴀᴛʜᴇᴜ, known as Manuel de Falla, was born on November 23, 1876, at Cadiz, Spain. His father's family came from Borja, or Borgia, near Grandía; and his mother's family originated in Southern Catalonia. Thus by birth he inherited two distinct sets of Spanish qualities and consequently, became more genuinely "Spanish."

His mother taught him to play the piano when he was quite young, and to her great delight, when he was nine years old, he played Haydn's *Seven Last Words of Christ*, as a duet, with her at the Church of San Francisco at Cadiz. This had been specially written for the Church of La Cueva at Cadiz and has since become a traditional part of the Good Friday Service in several other Cadiz churches.

Manuel soon decided that he did not want to become a virtuoso-pianist but a composer. With this in mind, he studied musical theory and harmony with two Cadiz musicians. Then at seventeen, he heard a symphony for the first time and his fate was sealed. He would become a composer! He devoured Wagner's scores; he began to write chamber music for a group that met frequently at a local violoncellist's home; and his own ambition was to go to Paris to study!

Alas, he did not have the funds to go there. But determined to find a way, he set about composing—what he supposed would bring certain financial rewards—a zarzuela, or comic-opera. Though this was practically the only

151

type of music in vogue at the time, neither of his efforts in this style met with success: in fact, one was never even produced.

But it so happened that—though Spain had had no major composer in over two hundred years—there was at that time, at Madrid, an eminent composer, Felipe Pedrell, then in his sixties, who had been devoting his life to a revival of Spanish musical culture. Falla decided to go to him for guidance, and as a result both he and Spanish music benefited.

Falla studied composition with Pedrell for about three years and during that time "grew up" in his own creative ability. Influenced by Pedrell, he became convinced that each country should base its "composed" music on the *spirit* of its folk-music—not copying or actually borrowing its themes, but imbibing its spirit.

At the same time he studied the piano under José Trago, and through the encouragement of both teachers, he entered two musical contests—winning both of them! In 1905 he won the Madrid Academy of Art Award with his two-act lyric or singing drama, *Life is Short;* and the same year he won the Ortiz y Cussó Prize for pianists.

Following these events, he taught piano in Madrid for two years. Then in the summer of 1907 his dream came true—he went to Paris. He went for a seven-day visit and stayed for seven years!

Soon after his arrival, he met Claude Debussy, Maurice Ravel and Paul Dukas; and this meeting with Debussy, according to Falla's own words was the turning point in his career. Pedrell had directed his attention to the Spanish spirit, but Debussy, though a Frenchman, made him *feel* it. And to Debussy, finely tuned to the popular Spanish music by instinct rather than by birth, Falla appeared as the realization of his dreams.

In 1908 Falla's own genius thus stimulated, burst forth in his "symphonic impressions" called *Nights in the Gardens of Spain.* This composition, written for piano and orchestra, was not finished until 1916, but its appearance established Falla as the leading Spanish composer of his day. The *Nights,* magically expressive of the music of Andalucía, that part of Spain generally considered most typically Spanish, in fact most oriental, is not a conventional

152

piano concerto. Though the piano plays a brilliant rôle, it does so as a member of the orchestra rather than as a solo instrument.

Meanwhile in 1908, Ricardo Viñes, the pianist famous for his interpretation of Ravel's music, played Falla's Four Spanish Pieces for piano at a Société Nationale de Musique concert. And in 1911 Falla made his London debut as a pianist in these pieces.

Then in 1913 Falla returned to Spain where on November 14, his lyric drama, *Life is Short,* was given at Madrid. Settling down there, he wrote his brilliant ballet-pantomime, *Wedded By Witchcraft,* based on a folk-tale, known in many countries, about the ghost of a dead lover always returning at the right moment to drive away a rival suitor. *Wedded by Witchcraft* was first given in 1915 at Madrid. Only a ballet performance of the work fully reveals its intricate mesh of contrasting rhythms, but some of this quality can be appreciated in the "Ritual Fire-dance" from it, often played as a piano solo.

Falla's next important work was his ballet, *The Three Cornered Hat,* performed by the Diaghilev Ballet on July 22, 1919, in London. Leonide Massine created the rôle of the miller in this amusing ballet which has become increasingly popular.

This same year Falla composed his Fantasía Bética for the piano and dedicated it to Artur Rubinstein. In it he employed the "feeling" of the Spanish guitar, which, alchemized by Falla's peculiar genius, becomes uniquely effective.

Still another work began to occupy his mind in 1919—*The Puppet-Show*— a "musical and scenic adaptation" from an episode in Cervantes' *Don Quixote.* Meanwhile having decided to move to Granada, in 1920, he divided his time between work on *The Puppet-Show* and house-hunting. Before finding his Granada haven, however, his composing was interrupted for a time by concert-giving, including one concert given in London in 1921 when he appeared with great success as soloist in his *Nights in the Gardens of Spain.*

That fall he found his Granada home after some difficulty and there he worked on *The Puppet-Show* and organized a festival of cante hondo, a type

153

of Andalusian folk-song. Despite these varied activities, Falla finished *The Puppet-Show* in time for a concert performance of it at Seville on March 23, 1923. In June it was given a brilliant performance by Princess de Polignac's puppets, and the following year it was performed five times at Bristol, England. Serious humor, hovering over beautiful and rhythmic language set to music, makes of *The Puppet-Show* an exciting affair.

Falla's next composition, his Harpsichord Concerto continued along the path he had begun to pursue in *The Puppet-Show*. Less typically "Spanish" in the accepted sense, it glitters and sparkles with an inner Spanish quality, peculiar to the period in the 18th century, when Domenico Scarlatti lived long in Spain, and, though Italian by birth wrote "Spanish" music.

After appearing as soloist in the Harpsichord Concerto in London in June 1927, Falla began work on a large composition for solo singers, chorus and orchestra, based on the *Atlantida*, a Catalan epic poem.

Reserved by nature, Falla kept more and more close to his work though he gave occasional concerts. In 1930 he conducted a festival of his own music at Salle Pleyel in Paris. But even in 1936, when the Civil War disrupted Spain, he remained rooted to his Granada home near the Alhambra. In 1938 he was named President of the Institute of Spain.

He was persuaded to go to Buenos Aires, in the fall of 1939, to conduct concerts. There in South America high up in the Argentine Andes at Villa Paz near Cordoba, Falla sought refuge from a war-maddened world. And there he continued to work on his *Atlantida*. Carlton Smith, an American music critic, who spent a holiday with him, described his host as delicate and frail in appearance with fire underneath.

This too, describes Falla's music—its lines finely and delicately chiseled, its substance alive with conflicting melodies and rhythms—genuinely Spanish in spirit!

RESPIGHI

Courtesy of "Musical Courier"

OTTORINO RESPIGHI

Sight and Sound of Rome

BORN 1879—DIED 1936

Oттовтно Respіghі was born in sunny Italy at Bologna on July 9, 1879. This was the year that Richard Wagner finished the skeleton-score of *Parsifal;* Anton Dvořák's music was just making itself known in the world; and Maurice Ravel was then a boy of five. Ottorino was the son of Giuseppe and Erminie Putti Respighi—the, names alone enough to give him a musical start in life. And just the fact that he was born in Italy meant that music and living went hand in hand.

When he was twelve years old he enrolled at the Musical Lyceum of Bologna where he specialized in the violin under Professor Frederico Sarti. Later he studied composition with Luigi Torchi and Giuseppe Martucci. Though he was to be tempted, later, by various "moderns" and colorists in music, he never lost contact with this formal training.

In 1899 Respighi was granted a diploma in violin, and in the following June he made his debut as a composer with the *Variazioni sinfoniche.* Now as an honest-to-goodness musician, off he went to far away Russia where he played first viola in the orchestra of the St. Petersburg Opera.

Arrived in St. Petersburg, he did the most natural thing in the world: he began to study composition and orchestration with Rimsky-Korsakov. He received his diploma in composition with the *Preludio Corale, e Fuga,* and from then on his music showed definite traces of Rimsky-Korsakov's teaching.

Respighi's next training came from Max Bruch, with whom Ralph Vaughan

Williams studied, in Berlin. Then gradually his compositions found a place on the concert stage: his piano concerto was performed at the Musical Lyceum at Bologna; his *Noturrno* for orchestra was given at the Metropolitan in New York City; and *Re Engo*, a comic-opera, was produced at Bologna. In 1910 his opera, *Semirama*, definitely influenced by hearing Richard Strauss' opera, *Salome*, was given its first performance at the Teatro Comunale in Bologna.

Meanwhile Respighi acted as pianist at the singing school of Etelka Gardini-Gerster in Berlin and appeared in many concerts both as violinist and viola-player.

In 1913 he was appointed instructor in composition by the Academy of Saint Cecilia in Rome, a turn of events that helped to make him a happy and productive man. His classes in composition became very popular and he composed his best music in the "Rome" years. One work—his symphonic poem, *The Fountains of Rome*—remains a monument to his oneness with his chosen city.

The Fountains of Rome, given its first performance under A. Guarnieri at the Augusteo in Rome on March 11, 1916, is a tone-picture of four of Rome's fountains at the hour best suited to bring out the beauty of each. The poem opens with *The Fountain of Valle Guilia at Dawn*—expressing a country scene with the sound of cattle passing and disappearing into the misty freshness of a Roman dawn. The second part suggests *The Triton Fountain at Dawn*—wide awake and joyous. Next comes *The Fountain of Trevi at Mid-day*—solemn and triumphant. And last, *The Villa Medici Fountain at Sunset*—with a touch of sunset's sadness in the music—followed by a feeling of peace.

In 1919 Respighi married one of his pupils, Elsa Olivieri-Sangiacomo, an accomplished composer and singer. Continuing at his teaching post, he was made director of the Royal Conservatory of Music of Saint Cecilia in 1923, but at the end of two years he gave it up—keeping only a course in advanced composition—in order to devote himself to composing and concert-giving.

Meanwhile in 1924, his symphonic poem, *The Pines of Rome* had been given its first performance at the Augusteo under the direction of Bernardino Molinari. Once again Rome served as his inspiration. *The Pines of Rome,* divided into four parts and played without a pause, expresses in music what the ancient pine trees of Rome have seen and remembered. The first part, *The Pines of the Villa Borghese*, remains in the present—the trees looking fondly down upon happy children at play. *The Pines Near a Catacomb* produces an entirely different scene—moody, gloomy and mysterious—ending with the sound of a trumpet in the distance. Then comes *The Pines of the Janiculum*—the hill-top pines—raising their arms to heaven in the moonlight, to a nightingale's song—breaking through the mists to the dawn. And, finally, *Pines of the Appian Way*—remembering marching soldiers, flying banners and blaring trumpets, home triumphant—ending in a blare of orchestral glory!

And still a third symphonic work, *Roman Festivals*, composed in 1928, gives further musical impressions of Rome. The first part *Circus Maximus*, paints a picture in music of an ancient circus mob—brutal and relentless. The second part, *The Jubilee*, tells the story of plodding pilgrims approaching the eternal city—"Rome! Rome!" they cry with joy and thanksgiving as the bells of Rome bid them welcome. The third section, *The October Festival*, waxes mellow with the fullness of harvest. And the poem closes with *The Epiphany*, picturing a ceremonial feast, ending in peasant dances, barrel-organ playing and general confusion.

Meanwhile Respighi had been growing more and more interested in Gregorian music, an interest that showed plainly in some of his works. Later, he turned to opera-writing, as almost every Italian composer is certain to do eventually.

In 1932 he went on a concert-tour in America after which he was nominated to the Royal Academy of Italy. Opera-writing then occupied him more and more, until after a long illness, he died on March 23, 1936 at his villa "I Pini" in Rome.

He was buried among the honored-ones at his birthplace, Bologna. And his last opera, *Lucrezia*, completed by his widow, Elsa Olivieri-Sangiacomo Respighi, was performed on February 24, 1937, at La Scala in Milan.

Ottorino Respighi—a name that brings to mind set forms of orchestral color—picturing in music the sights, the sounds and the spirit of Rome!

BARTÓK

BÉLA BARTÓK

Hungarian Composer and Folk-Song Collector

BORN 1881

Béla Bartók was born on March 25, 1881, at Nagy Szent Miklós in the district of Torontal in Greater Hungary. Lying in the path of invading countries for ten centuries, Hungary had again and again gathered new elements into her folklore. Béla Bartók was destined to help separate the true from the false by gathering together thousands of *genuine* Hungarian folk-tunes.

Béla's father, Director of the School of Agriculture, was also an able amateur musician. The story goes that—though a pianist, when a 'cellist was needed in an orchestra that he organized—he learned to play the violoncello to remedy the situation. Still more inventive and accommodating, he also wrote music for the orchestra to play.

Unfortunately when Béla was eight years old his father died, and the task of supporting and educating the young boy fell on his mother. Almost at once she moved to Nagy-Szöllös where she secured a teaching position; and she later went to Besterce for the same reason.

Meanwhile she gave Béla piano lessons. He not only showed promise of becoming a good pianist, but he began to write little piano pieces; and at ten he made his public debut as both composer and pianist. Madame Bartók then made up her mind to move to Pressburg where Béla might have proper musical training.

Settled in Pressburg, Béla began to study piano and composition with

163

Laszlo Erkel who was a son of Ferenč Erkel, regarded as the "Father of Modern Hungarian Music."

Eagerly devoting himself to music, in addition to his studies, he attended concerts of the St. Martin Music Society, played in chamber music groups and wrote a fair amount of piano music. His education of this period was classic in nature, ranging from Bach to Brahms, and in truth, his first piano compositions strongly show the Brahms influence.

During this time he made the acquaintance of Ernst von Dohnányi, a young Hungarian composer, four years his senior. And through Dohnányi's influence, young Bartók, after finishing his Pressburg schooling, went to the Budapest Conservatory where he studied piano with István Thomán, a pupil of Liszt, and composition with Hans Koessler.

While a student at the Conservatory, Bartók, becoming familiar with the music of Wagner and Liszt, was freed from his over-closeness to Brahms. But at the same time, finding no congenial stimulus to his own nature, he wrote practically no music for two years. Meanwhile his skill as a pianist won enthusiastic praise from his classmates.

"Béla makes the piano talk!"

And strangely enough, this quality of communicating or expressing an idea, appeared later in his own music, once he had got into his stride.

At about the time that he left the Conservatory Bartók heard a performance of Richard Strauss's *Thus Spake Zarathustra*. Though the audience was indignantly opposed to it, Bartók, vastly impressed, began to study the Strauss scores. And he later gave a brilliant performance of Strauss's *Ein Heldenleben*, on the piano at a concert in Vienna.

But the "Strauss" period was a short one. Bartók was becoming more and more national-minded, and his first large orchestral work, the *Kossuth* Symphony, abounds in patriotic feeling. Performed by the Budapest Philharmonic the year Bartók left the Conservatory, it met with tremendous success. And when Bartók appeared in Hungarian folk-costume at the end of the performance, he was given an ovation.

Hans Richter conducted the *Kossuth* Symphony a month later for the Manchester Philharmonic Society in England. At about the same time Bartók's unpublished Violin Sonata was played in Vienna; he appeared as soloist in his own Piano Quintet with the Prill Quartet in Budapest; and some of his music was being published. This included the first two piano Rhapsodies, some small piano pieces and songs, followed by the first.Suite for orchestra.

Meanwhile Bartók had gained fresh inspiration from traveling through the byways of Hungary with his friend Zoltán Kodály. Both young musicians became convinced that the true Hungarian folk-spirit had been buried beneath the better-known Slovak and gypsy element in their country's music. In 1906 Bartók, in collaboration with Kodály published Twenty Hungarian Folk-Songs for voice and piano accompaniment; and thereafter Bartók's own music reflected the discovery of this genuine Hungarian spirit.

He became Professor of Pianoforte at the Royal Academy of Music at Budapest in 1907. Then largely through Kodály's influence, he began to study the music of such modern western composers as Debussy and Stravinsky. Wholly unfamiliar to Hungarian audiences, this "new music" found favor with Bartók, for certain of its qualities were his by nature.

His individual style revealed itself magnificently in the First String Quartet, written in 1908. Delicate melodic outline combined with a tender and passionate spirit, give a special spiritual quality to this work, stamping it—the *real* Bartók.

Following this string quartet came several sets of piano pieces, some of which remain the best known of Bartók's music. They are: the *Bagatelles*, the *Roumanian Dances*, *Burlesques*, *Elegies*, the *Esquisses*, the *Ten Easy Pieces* and four volumes *Children's Pieces*. There is in most of them an illusive charm and a simplicity, resulting from an inner intensity that shines through crystal-clear from composer to listener.

Though some of Bartók's music was now being performed, it was not yet genuinely appreciated. Due to this lack of recognition, he turned more and more to folk-study. In 1911 he and Kodály founded the New Hungarian Musical Society in Budapest and traveled further afield for folk-tunes. Then in 1913 Bartók went to Africa to study the music of the Arabs at Biskra, returning with two hundred tunes. The same year his collection of folk-songs from the district of Bihar was published.

165

In 1917 Hungary began to appreciate the music of her native son. His piano pieces began to be known, the Philharmonic Society gave successful concerts of his works and the Women's Choral Society of Budapest sang his folk-songs. That spring his ballet-pantomime, *The Wooden Prince,* was successfully given at the Royal Hungarian Opera House. And when his opera, *Bluebeard's Castle,* written seven years before had been successfully produced, Bartók was truly regarded as Hungary's leading composer!

Though the War and revolution in Hungary influenced his career, Bartók continued to compose; and immediately following the War, his music began to be played more and more throughout the world. He was given an ovation at a concert of the Revue Musicale at Paris in 1922; and the following year at a grand music festival celebrating the fiftieth anniversary of Buda's union with Pest, his *Dance Suite* was performed for the first time. Immediately successful, it was performed in Germany fifty times in one year.

Meanwhile Bartók helped organize the International Society for Contemporary Music. And his music beginning with the First Violin Sonata, was played at most of the societies' annual festivals, held thereafter.

Bartók's later works, combining an individual style, with the unique Hungarian rhythmic quality, produced music of universal significance. They include the two Violin and Piano Sonatas; the Third, Fourth and Fifth String Quartets; his second Piano Concerto; Music for strings, percussion and celesta; Music for Two Pianos and Percussion; and his choral work, *Cantata Profana.*

Frail in appearance like Falla, and also strengthened by some inner fire, Bartók, too, fled from the horrors of a second great war in one century, to America where he gave concerts and composed.

Hungarian by heritage, but universal in spirit, Bartók's music carries promise of joining that of the Immortals.

STRAVINSKY

IGOR STRAVINSKY

Original! Russian! Modern!

BORN 1882

On JUNE 17, 1882, there was born at Oranienbaum, near St. Petersburg, in Russia, the "Composer of Today"—Igor Stravinsky. For in his own words, he did not live for yesterday or tomorrow, but for the day in hand. Born on St. Igor's day, according to the Russian calendar, he was named "Igor," thereby beginning the first day of his life according to this day-in-hand philosophy.

Though his father was a leading bass singer of the Imperial Opera in St. Petersburg, Igor's parents did not plan a musical career for their son. Nevertheless, music attracted him from the time he was quite young. And one day when he cleverly imitated the singing of a group of village women on their way home from work, his father remarked, "You have a true ear."

This bit of encouragement marks the starting point of his musical career. From then on, he thought of himself as a musician.

Beginning to take piano lessons when he was nine, he learned to read music with no difficulty. That accomplished, he began to improvise at the piano for hours at a time. And when he became a composer this was the way in which he created a great deal of his music.

At the same time he devoured the opera scores in his father's library and to his great delight, when taken to the opera for the first time, what did he see but Glinka's *A Life for the Tsar!* Why! he already knew it from having read and played the score. Hearing it with a full orchestra—the first orchestra he ever heard—was an experience that he never forgot.

Shortly afterward he attended the fiftieth anniversary performance of Glinka's opera *Russlan and Ludmilla,* in which his father sang the bass-rôle. Once again the occasion proved memorable, for during the intermission, Igor caught a glimpse of Peter Ilyitch Tchaikovsky, who had recently conducted the first performance of his "Pathetic" Symphony. Two weeks later Igor's mother took him to a concert at which this work was performed as a memorial to its composer who had suddenly died. And growing more and more fond of Tchaikovsky's music, Igor, later, looked back with gratitude to that one glimpse of his idol.

Despite Igor's association with things musical—his piano playing, score-reading and concert-going, to which he had added the study of counterpoint "for fun"—his parents insisted upon his going to the University of St. Petersburg to study law. It so happened that Rimsky-Korsakov's youngest son was at the University, and he and Igor became good friends. Then in the summer of 1902 when Rimsky-Korsakov took his family to Heidelberg to be near his son, Andrei, who was studying in Germany, the Stravinskys happened to be staying at Wildungen, nearby, for Igor's father's health. Igor, killing two birds with one stone, dashed over to Heidelberg to see his classmate and to consult Rimsky-Korsakov about his career. Though Rimsky-Korsakov was not exactly enthusiastic over young Stravinsky's compositions, he did encourage him to continue his harmony and counterpoint studies. And he recommended, as a teacher, one of his own advanced pupils.

Meanwhile Igor's father having died, young Stravinsky set about establishing an independent life for himself among congenial friends, including Sergei Diaghilev who proved so important in his career. Diaghilev had just started a modern review called *The World of Art;* the air was astir with artistic revolt, and Stravinsky was in his element! At the same time he made the acquaintance of the music of several French composers—César Franck, Debussy, Chabrier and others. New worlds stretched before him.

Beginning his first piano sonata, and coming upon snags that he could not unravel, Stravinsky consulted Rimsky-Korsakov. And Rimsky-Korsakov became Stravinsky's teacher in spite of himself. The sonata was finished under his supervision; form and composition-study went hand-in-hand; and then Rimsky-Korsakov assigned pages of his own operas for Stravinsky to score. When finished, Rimsky-Korsakov compared them with his own and explained why he had scored differently in places. At other times he gave his pupil a Beethoven sonata or a Schubert quartet to orchestrate. Then the moment came when Rimsky-Korsakov permitted Stravinsky to start his first symphony, remembering, perhaps, his own excitement when writing *Russia's* first symphony!

In January 1906, Stravinsky, having left the University, and having gained sure knowledge of the course he was to follow, married his second cousin, Nadejda Soulima. Continuing his studies with Rimsky-Korsakov, he finished the first symphony in 1907 and dedicated it to his teacher. He then wrote a little suite for voice and orchestra, *Faune et Bergère*, which Rimsky-Korsakov arranged to be played for a private audience by Court orchestra. Later, it was given publicly at one of the famous Belaiev concerts.

Shortly afterward, Stravinsky interrupted some larger works to compose his symphonic poem, *Fireworks*, to celebrate the marriage of Rimsky-Korsakov's daughter. Finishing it in six weeks, he sent off the score, but alas, Rimsky-Korsakov died before the package arrived. Deeply moved, Stravinsky wrote a *Funeral Chant* in his memory and it, also, was performed at a Belaiev concert.

On February 6, 1909, Stravinsky's *Fantastic* Scherzo was given at a Siloti concert in St. Petersburg. Little did he know that this event would direct his entire career! Sergei Diaghilev, impressed with the music, commissioned him to orchestrate two of the Chopin pieces of music for the ballet, *Les Sylphides*, to be given in Paris that spring. Such was the beginning of an association—lasting for twenty years—that resulted in the music we think of as—Stravinsky!

The first original ballet to develop from this dynamic combination was *The Firebird*. Finished on May 18, 1910, it was given its first performance by the Russian Ballet under Diaghilev on June the 25th in Paris. *The Firebird*, based on a Russian fairy tale, definitely established Stravinsky in the world of modern music. Musically related to Rimsky-Korsakov's teaching, it, nevertheless, contained the seeds of the later, revolutionary Stravinsky—destined to burst full-blown in *Petroushka*.

Let us see how *Petroushka* came about. While Stravinsky was finishing *The Firebird*, a tiny bit of his mind began to dream of other matters. A primitive world appeared as a vision in which a young girl was dancing herself to death as a sacrifice to the birth of spring. The subject fascinated him. Diaghilev was equally enthusiastic. But the *Sacre du Printemps*, or *Rite of Spring*, as it was eventually called, would be taxing to his energies, so, before he began this exacting task, he would write, for his own enjoyment, a concert piece in which the piano and the orchestra fought, one with the other.

That is how *Petroushka* came into being. And that is how the famous "Petroushka chord"—with its two keys playing together—was born, destined to strike a match that fired a whole new world of music. Stravinsky pictured a puppet, suddenly come to life, exasperating the orchestra, with dynamic antics on the piano, answered by loud trumpet blasts from the orchestra, until, at the climax of a terrific battle of sound, the puppet crumples into a heap.

When the piece was finished, Stravinsky was amazed at his own creation. What would he call this pitiful creature? Then, one day, the name stood before him—"Petroushka."

"Of course, why didn't I think of that before? He is 'Petroushka'—the luckless puppet-hero of every land."

Diaghilev, once he had recovered from Stravinsky's switching to *Petroushka*, was delighted with the new piece. Stravinsky must make a whole ballet of it! And thus, *Petroushka*, set in the midst of a crowded fair, with its booths, magician and miniature theater, came into being. Thus, Petroushka, endowed with life, struggles frantically for the dancer, his loved one, and in the end falls dead at the hands of his rival.

Finished in Rome, *Petroushka* was given its first performance by Diaghilev at Paris on June 13, 1911. Nijinsky created the rôle of Petroushka, and Karsavina, that of the dancer—both to Stravinsky's complete satisfaction and the audience's spontaneous delight.

Soon afterward, Stravinsky left for Oustilong, his Russian estate, where the *Rite of Spring* got under way. Finished at Clarens, Switzerland, in March 1913, it was given its first performance by the Russian ballet at the opening of the Théâtre des Champs-Élysées in Paris. Not since the memorable spring of 1861, when the Jockey Club played such havoc with Wagner's *Tannhaüser*, had there been such a scandalous scene. The strange, new sound of the music, beginning with a bassoon solo, and building relentlessly into an abandoned frenzy, horrified the audience. Shouts, protests, and laughter greeted Stravinsky's ears as he dashed from the theater.

But a year later when it was given with *Petroushka* in a concert performance, it met with warm approval from critics and audience.

The spring of 1914, Stravinsky went to Russia for what proved to be his last visit. Despite the rumblings of war, and his anxiety over them, he buried himself in the study of Russian folk-songs, falling captive to the cadence of their words. Returning to Switzerland, he used some of these songs in three choral works that paved the way for his unique cantata, *Les Noces*. In addition to the striking array of voices, *Les Noces* is scored for four pianos and seventeen percussion instruments. Begun in 1915, it was not completely scored until 1923, when Diaghilev produced it in Paris.

Meanwhile Stravinsky composed *Renard*, a burlesque-opera based on Russian folklore, three songs for children, in Russian style, and some choruses, also in the Russian spirit.

Then in the spring of 1917, he had an opportunity to compose something Russian "on the spot." A gala performance of the Russian Ballet was being given in Rome, and since, shortly before, the Russian Revolution had forced the Tsar to abdicate his throne, it was not fitting to open a performance, as had been the custom, with the Russian National Anthem, *God Save the Tsar*.

"Let's use a Russian folk-song," suggested Diaghilev. "The *Volga Boat Song*, perhaps."

"Good," said Stravinsky, "but how about a score for the orchestra?"

"You will attend to that," exclaimed Diaghilev. And so he did. Sitting at the piano at a friend's apartment, he worked all night, dictating the orchestration chord by chord. After one rehearsal the following morning, it took its triumphant place in the evening's performance.

War, Revolution, Change, having occurred under his very nose, Stravinsky true to his nature, faced facts. He would write smaller works, suitable for modern production. Combining thought with action, and still concerned with Russian folklore, he chose to tell, in music, a Russian tale about a deserting soldier and the devil. Calling it *Histoire du Soldat,* he revealed the story by means of a narrator, four actors and *seven* instruments—the star of the cast, undoubtedly the percussion with its dynamic rhythm. At its first performance in Lausanne on September 28, 1918, a performance particularly dear to Stravinsky, Ernest Ansermet, the conductor, took leading honors.

The *Soldat* finished, Stravinsky turned to a new field of music—jazz. It fascinated him. Poring over stacks of this popular music with its alluring rhythm, while he was recovering from a siege of influenza, he decided to write a jazz concert piece. This turned out to be his *Ragtime* for eleven instruments.

Then Diaghilev commissioned him to write a ballet based on music of the early Italian composer, Pergolesi. Having always admired Pergolesi's Neapolitan music, Stravinsky set about his task with passionate devotion. *Pulcinella,* he called his one-act ballet, and it was produced by Diaghilev at Paris in the spring of 1920.

After finishing his little opera, *Mavra,* dedicated to the memory of Pushkin, Glinka and Tchaikovsky, Stravinsky bade good-by to Russian subjects. More and more, he turned to the objective in music, the classic style of composition. In this manner, he wrote the *Octet* for wind instruments, a Concerto for piano and orchestra of wind instruments, a *Serenade* for piano, and an oratorio, *Oedipus Rex.* Searching for the most impersonal language in which to express this choral work, he had the text translated into medieval Latin.

Meanwhile Stravinsky had made his first American tour, and while there, he was commissioned by Elizabeth Sprague Coolidge to write a ballet suite. Returning to Europe, he carried out this commission in the form of an ancient dance suite, calling it *Apollon Musagètes.*

Then came his composition, *Le Baiser de la Fée,* a ballet-allegory, inspired by Tchaikovsky's music. In 1929 he wrote his *Capriccio* for piano and orchestra; and on August 15, 1930, he completed his *Symphony of Psalms*, dedicated "to the Glory of God," and written to celebrate the fiftieth anniversary of the Boston Symphony Orchestra. The *Symphony of Psalms* is scored for chorus and orchestra without violins or violas, for Stravinsky was determined to rule out possibilities of over-expression in tone color.

In 1931, he wrote his Violin Concerto and in the following year, a suite for Violin and Piano called Duo Concertant. His ballet, *Persephone*, commissioned by Ida Rubinstein, was given its first performance at Paris on April 30, 1934; and during the following year, he wrote a Concerto for two pianos, with orchestral accompaniment.

Card Party, "a ballet in three deals," based on a poker game, was performed at the Metropolitan Opera House in New York while Stravinsky was touring America in 1937. The next year, he wrote a Concerto for sixteen instruments, performed in Washington under the title *Dumbarton Oaks*, named after the estate of a Washington music lover. In 1940 his Symphony in C was given its first performance by the Chicago Symphony Orchestra to celebrate the orchestra's fiftieth anniversary.

Stravinsky, born in Russia, living long in Switzerland, and having become a French citizen, began in 1939, to make his home in America. At Harvard University, he occupied the Charles Eliot Norton Chair of Poetics; and while intellectually, he upheld the dignity of this title, emotionally, he became entranced with America's swing music—"music of the people"—he called it.

Percussion. A staccato moment—caught up in bold diagonal rhythm—primitive and modern—Stravinsky!

GRIFFES

CHARLES TOMLINSON GRIFFES

American Tone-painter

BORN 1884—DIED 1920

Charles Tomlinson Griffes, destined in his short life to create music of lingering beauty, was born on September 17, 1884, in Elmira, New York. Claude Debussy—his spiritual brother, in a sense—had been born twenty-two years before in France, and Arnold Schoenberg—destined to affect the cause of his later music—was exactly ten.

Charles, the third in a family of five, grew up in a home in which literature, music and art were a part of each day's living. His father, Wilbur Griffes, a successful business man, and his mother, also, enjoyed the sound of music, popping up in various parts of the house, as each member of the family learned to play a musical instrument. The eldest daughter played the violin, the second one, the piano. And when the latter became a piano teacher, Charles Tomlinson was one of her first pupils.

From an early age, Charles read everything that he could get his hands on; and he chose his friends, not, because they "lived next door," or, played on the baseball team, but because they shared his interest in music and literature. Edgar Allan Poe was one of his favorite authors; and later, Lefcadio Hearn, who wrote with rare sensitivity on the Orient, found favor with him.

Miss Mary Broughton followed his sister as piano teacher, and it was she who encouraged him to make music his profession. At her advice, he set out for Berlin when he was nineteen years old, in order to prepare himself for a concert-pianist's career.

Arrived there, he studied piano first with Ernst Jedliczka and later with Gottfried Gallston. At the same time, he studied musical theory from Wilhelm Klatte and Max Julius Loewengard; and composition from Phillip Rüfer and Englebert Humperdinck.

Humperdinck, the composer of *Haensel and Gretel*, contributed greatly to Griffes' decision to become a composer. And his German studies, in general, determined the choice of his first works to be published—settings to five German poems.

After teaching for several years in Berlin, Griffes returned to America where he accepted a position as piano teacher, organist and choir master at the Hackley School for Boys at Tarrytown, New York.

There it was possible for him to combine teaching with composition. And as time and distance separated him from the German influence, he "came to himself" in growing nearer to the French School of Impressionism. His Three Tone Pictures for piano illustrate this tendency. They are: *The Veil of Dreams, The Night Winds* and *The Lake at Evening*—"I hear lake water lapping with low sounds by the shore," wrote the poet, William Butler Yeats, and Griffes translated the words into music that truly sounds like the rippling of a lake.

Griffes, always seeking to express a feeling and an atmosphere, often broke with traditional methods, but never for the sake of experimentation itself. For instance, in the *Barcarolle* from his Fantasy Pieces, he used the whole-tone scale to help express the mystery of the sea.

The next set of piano pieces—Roman Sketches—established his individuality as a composer, though this was not recognized in his lifetime. The pieces in this group consist of: *Clouds, The Fountain of the Acqua Paola, Nightfall* and *The White Peacock*. In each, the "right" chords are used to express the exact feeling—as the music struts with the vain peacock, becomes quiet with evening, shimmers with the rise and fall of the fountain, and soars aloft with the clouds in the last piece.

Griffes then wrote Three Poems for voice and piano, fairly radical in treatment, and followed them with *Five Poems of Ancient China and Japan*. In

180

these, with the help of the five- and six-tone scale, he created an authentic Oriental atmosphere, and at the same time, genuinely beautiful music.

Then came the splendid Three Poems by Fiona MacLeod in musical settings, consisting of: *The Lament of Ian the Proud, Thy Dark Eyes to Mine,* and *Rose of the Night.* Following these, Griffes composed one of his most delightful songs, *An Old Song Re-Sung,* to a poem by John Masefield.

In his Piano Sonata, Griffes showed kinship with the "moderns," though even in it, he remained himself. Then he wrote the lovely Poem for Flute and Orchestra, for his friend, Georges Barrère. But the work, destined to bring him greatest renown, and ironically, the one that contributed to the illness that caused his death, was the tone-poem *The Pleasure Dome of Kubla Khan.*

The Boston Symphony Orchestra accepted, for performance, this tone-poem based on Coleridge's lines describing the "stately pleasure dome . . ."; and Griffes set to work at once to prepare the parts for rehearsal. The task proved too great for his health, already weakened by overwork. He fell ill with pneumonia, and during his illness, word came to him of the triumph of *The Pleasure Dome of Kubla Khan.*

Requests for permission to perform his works poured in from orchestras and various cities. Fame and recognition had finally come to him, but alas, it was not in the stars that he enjoy the experience, for he died in New York on April 8, 1920. And America lost, early, a developing artist.

Charles Tomlinson Griffes, creating—in pastel sounds—music of exquisite beauty, sometimes strange, but always lovely—always PICTURES.

PROKOFIEV

Courtesy of "Musical Courier"

SERGEI SERGEIVITCH PROKOFIEV

Puck in Music!

BORN 1891

Sᴇʀɢᴇɪ Sᴇʀɢᴇɪᴠɪᴛᴄʜ Pʀᴏᴋᴏғɪᴇᴠ was born two years and a whole half-century after the birth of Modest Mussorgsky in the village of Sontzovka, in the Ekaterinoslav government of Russia on April 23, 1891. His father directed a large estate, owned by the family for whom the village was named. And his mother—who enjoyed playing the piano, particularly Chopin and Beethoven—contributed to her son's early liking for good music.

Hearing his family discuss a famine in India, Sergei, when he was five and a half years old, slipped away to the piano and made up a little piece on the spot, calling it "The Hindu Gallop." Though he played it in a key that called for an occasional B flat, Sergei always left this note out, for he was frightened to death of the black keys!

At the end of another six months, he was not only composing music but he was putting it down on paper. And when he was nine, he wrote an-honest-to-goodness opera called *The Giant*, performed at his uncle's estate that same summer. Thus encouraged, he started a much more elaborate opera, *On The Desert Island*, but it got no further than the overture.

This overture, however, served a worthy purpose, for when young Sergei played it for Sergei Taneiev in Moscow, Taneiev advised him to take up a regular course of harmony and composition.

Thus at eleven, young Prokofiev began to study music in earnest. His first teacher, Reinhold Glière, proved to have been a good choice; for recognizing

185

talent in the boy, Glière combined strict study with freedom in a way that avoided the dangers of over-discipline on a creative spirit. And before long, with Glière's help and encouragement, Sergei had written a symphony. Then in the following summer, he completed an opera based on Pushkin's *Feast During the Plague.*

In the spring of 1904, Sergei, at the advice of Alexander Glazounov, entered the St. Petersburg Conservatory. Carrying a folio, bulging with his compositions, and obviously talented, he was immediately accepted by Anatol Liadov in harmony and counterpoint, and by Rimsky-Korsakov in composition.

It was not long before Prokofiev was expressing himself in ways not approved at the Conservatory. His Peck's-Bad-Boy spirit could contain itself no longer. It bubbled forth in extremely original piano pieces, which he played on December 31, 1908, in St. Petersburg, at a concert of the Contemporary Music Society. The seventeen-year-old boy in his first public appearance, dazzled the audience, if not wholly with his talent, at least with his musical impudence!

That summer he composed another symphony. Then in the fall he began to study piano with Annette Essipov, and conducting under Nicholas Tcherepnin; and in 1909, he wrote his Sinfonietta, later revised, which pointed the way towards his individual style. During the following year he wrote two symphonic poems: *Rêves*, dedicated to Alexander Scriabin, and *Esquisse automnale* under the influence of Sergei Rachmaninov.

But it was with his First Piano Concerto, written in 1911, that the genuine Puckish-Prokofiev emerged. This served as his graduation piece from the St. Petersburg Conservatory. He played it on May 24, 1914, at the commencement exercises and received the first prize, a grand piano.

Meanwhile he had written two piano sonatas and many separate piano pieces, ten of which were published together as a suite. Also, some of his compositions had been publicly performed, usually, with Prokofiev as pianist.

In 1914, he composed his first major orchestral work, the primitive-sounding *Scythian Suite.* Given its first performance under Prokofiev in January 1916, it was immediately regarded as first-cousin of Stravinsky's

186

Rite of Spring. Then came the choral work for tenor, chorus and orchestra called *They Are Seven*, with its verbal inflection set against a background of "pure" dissonance.

And then somewhat in the spirit of a prankster, Prokofiev wrote his *Classical Symphony*, destined to be his most popular orchestral work. Fascinated with Mozart's singing qualities, Prokofiev asked himself, "how would Mozart write, were he alive today?" And the *Classical Symphony* was the result: truly Mozartean in melody and structure, with a dash of sophisticated harmony and turn-of-phrase at unexpected moments!

During 1915-16 Prokofiev composed his first "grown up" opera—*The Gamblers*—based on Dostoyevsky. In it, he sought new ways of expressing deep emotion, and at the same time, he drew on the realistic style of his forerunner, Modest Mussorgsky. Following that, came his ballet, *The Buffoon;* and his First Violin Concerto.

In the late summer of 1918, Prokofiev left Russia—then in the midst of want and disruption—by way of the Pacific, arriving in New York on September 18, 1918. During his stay in America, he appeared as pianist in various concerts of his work. Then on December 30, 1921, the Chicago Opera Company in presenting his fantastic opera, *Love for the Three Oranges*, had the distinction of giving the first Prokofiev opera production.

And once again, Diaghilev came into the life-story of a modern composer, when he gave Prokofiev's ballet, *The Buffoon*, known in French as *Chout*, at Paris in May 1921. Settling in Paris the following year, Prokofiev began to work in close association with Diaghilev. Then, though far away from his native land, Prokofiev though much about Russia, and in his ballet, *Le Pas d'Acier* or *The Steel Leap*, written in 1925, he attempted to evoke the spirit of industrial and social growth in Soviet Russia.

Shortly after Diaghilev produced *Le Pas d'Acier* in Paris on June 7, 1927, Prokofiev went on a concert tour to Russia where he was warmly welcomed. On returning to Paris he wrote the ballet, *L'Enfant Prodigue,* produced in 1929, the year of Diaghilev's death.

Meanwhile Prokofiev had made the acquaintance of the conductor, Sergei Koussevitsky, who performed many of his works, published some of his music as head of the Russian Publishing House in Paris, and later, commissioned Prokofiev to write a symphony for the fiftieth anniversary of the Boston Symphony Orchestra.

At the same time, Prokofiev continued to appear as pianist both in Europe and in America, giving the first performance of his Third Concerto with the Chicago Symphony Orchestra on December 16, 1921. He wrote his Fourth Concerto for Paul Wittgenstein, the one-armed pianist; and his Fifth Concerto was given by Prokofiev with the Berlin Philharmonic in the fall of 1932.

Prokofiev, in 1934, went home to Russia and identified himself with the Soviet Union. After a short period of readjustment to this new life, he wrote his Second Violin Concerto in G major, performed on December 1, 1935, in Madrid. In 1936, he wrote his *Russian Overture*, definitely national in feeling. And the following year, his Cantata based on speeches and writings by Marx, Lenin and Stalin—written to commemorate the twentieth anniversary of the Soviet Revolution—proclaimed his allegiance to Soviet thought.

Prokofiev, being so definitely a man of the twentieth century, found it natural to write music for the films. In the score for the motion picture, *Lieutenant Kijé*, he had an opportunity to write satirical music—music with a chuckle—to his heart's content. For the film, picturing a scene in Russia's past, *Alexander Nevsky*, Prokofiev provided music that combined his revolutionary modern qualities with a national Russian style, luxurious and colorful. Later, he used the *Alexander Nevsky* music in a cantata that was hailed with great enthusiasm by the Soviet public and press.

Following *Alexander Nevsky*, Prokofiev wrote a Soviet opera, *Simeon Kotko*, successfully produced in Moscow, in June 1940. That fall, he completed an opera based on Sheridan's *The Duenna*, and meanwhile he had finished the Sixth Piano Sonata, and written a ballet, *Romeo and Juliet*.

But despite these major works completed, and others in preparation, it took his fairy tale in music for children, *Peter and the Wolf*, to bring popular renown to Prokofiev. Given its first production at the Children's Theatre in Moscow on May 2, 1936, it later appeared in concerts, in ballet, in books, on records and over the air.

Peter and the Wolf tells a droll story of a Russian boy, disobeying the orders of his grandfather in an attempt to save the lives of his friends—the bird, the duck and the cat—from a wolf. Each character in the tale is represented by his own theme and his own instruments: Peter by the string quartet, the bird by the flute, the duck by the oboe, the cat by the clarinet in a low register, the grandfather by the bassoon, the wolf by the horns, and the shooting of the hunters by the kettle and bass drums.

This tale expresses the very essence of Prokofiev, sometimes more subtle, sometimes more melodious, but always with his "tongue in his cheek"—Puck in Music—Prokofiev!

GERSHWIN

Courtesy of American Society of Composers, Authors and Publishers

GEORGE GERSHWIN

Genius in Jazz

BORN 1898—DIED 1937

The twentieth century was just about to swing round the corner, when on September 26, 1898, in Brooklyn, New York, George Gershwin—destined to bring the American musical language to life—was born. Jerome Kern was thirteen years old and Irving Berlin was ten. Both were to kindle the spark of a singing America. Gershwin was to capture its soul.

His father, Morris Gershwin, had married lovely Rose Buskin when she was sixteen. Both had recently arrived in America from Russia, and both became eager young Americans. Soon after George's birth, they moved across the Brooklyn Bridge to the "sidewalks of New York" on the lower east side. And there George grew up—champion of the roller-skating fraternity—amid the rumble of the elevated overhead, the confusion of the traffic in the streets, and the clattering, clanging, cacophonous confusion of New York.

Music played but the average school-child rôle in George's early life—singing in assembly, listening to the Coney Island carrousel, attending a few educational concerts—with one exception: in later years he never recalled his penny arcade experience without a leap in his heart. He was six years old. Scuffing along, barefoot, outside a penny arcade in upper New York, he stopped. The automatic piano, inside, was leaping through the most fascinating melody. It jumped. It sang. It lived. He stood rooted to the spot.

193

And he never again heard Rubinstein's *Melody in F* without remembering that moment.

This was all very well for *listening*, but the young roller-skating, hockey-playing George had no patience with boys who practiced the piano or fiddled away on the violin. Such goings-on were for girls! Alas, some hidden desire to be doing that very thing must have been tormenting him, for no sooner had a second-hand piano found its way into the Gershwin home, than George was playing it! And though Ira, his elder brother, was immediately put to practicing scales, it was George, of all people, who, after making fascinating experiments at the keyboard, announced, "I want a music teacher."

Meanwhile another chance-experience had fired his imagination. At school one day, it had been announced that little Maxie Rosenweig would play the violin at an entertainment following the lunch recess. Poof! George couldn't be bothered with anything like that. But, all of a sudden, strains of Dvořák's famous *Humoresque* came floating down from the assembly room. "Why, it's beautiful!" George exclaimed to himself. And forthwith, he planted himself outside the school building, in the pouring rain, to wait for this amazing creature who could make the violin talk that way. But the young violinist, who later became well-known as Max Rosen, had vanished. Nothing daunted, George found out where he lived, and dashed there, only to be told that Max was not at home. His family, however, moved by the young admirer's distress, arranged a meeting for the boys and they became fast friends.

Max proved stimulating to him, but not overly encouraging, capping the climax one day by telling George that he should give up any idea of a musical career. "It isn't in you, Georgie. I can tell."

Once George had decided to take music lessons, he took them with a vengeance, first with three different women teachers, then with a man who put him through the paces of playing excerpts from the grand operas; and then through the help of a chance acquaintance, he found *his* teacher—in Charles Hambitzer. Born to music, and a thoroughly trained musician, Charles Hambitzer, once he had recovered from the shock of George's having learned many of the wrong things, found in his new pupil an inspiration for his own efforts. He even announced in a letter to his sister that he had a new pupil who was a genius. And thus it is Charles Hambitzer who can be credited with first visualizing George Gershwin, the composer.

Through Hambitzer, George entered a new world—his own. Chopin, Liszt, Debussy became his friends. Harmony—until then a complete mystery except for an instinctive feeling for certain chord combinations—came alive through music introduced by his new teacher. Hambitzer was wonderful! And George immediately found ten new pupils for him.

In addition to this piano instruction, young Gershwin, for short periods, studied harmony from Edward Kilenyi and Ruben Goldmark. But in harmony, composition and orchestration, he was, in the main, self-taught. From the beginning of his musical awakening, whenever he attended a concert, he *listened*; then when he got home, still *listening*, he would work it out on the piano—listening, learning, finding his way. And later, by *listening*, he succeeded in capturing in music, the speech, the spirit and the character of America.

Gershwin made his debut as pianist and composer in the spring of 1914 at an entertainment of the Finley Club. His brother, Ira, a member of the program committee, had arranged this exciting event which took place at Christadora House in New York City. Two of the numbers on the program read: Piano Solo by George Gershvin and Vocal Selections by Chas. Rose and George Gershvin—the "v" being Ira's way of spelling their name at that time. George's Piano Solo was a tango of his concocting and was more imitative than creative, but he was on the way!

Reading, writing, and arithmetic were never very exciting affairs for young Gershwin; but largely through Ira's influence, he was persuaded to enter the High School of Commerce. But what had all this putting-down of figures, black or red, to do with music? And when through a friend, he was introduced to the music publishing firm of Remick's, his fate was sealed! Though just a youngster, and inexperienced, he *could* play the piano, and he looked bright. Before he realized what had happened, he was working at fifteen dollars a week as a "song-plugger" in Tin Pan Alley.

Tin Pan Alley—Broadway, New York—the cradle of popular music. Here, songs of the day were born, polished and sent into the world. Here,

young men sat in tiny cubicles of rooms and pounded out numbers for singers, vaudeville performers, and producers—just like a carnival barker, singing his wares—"come buy . . . come make your fortune with this one."

And George Gershwin became a good "plugger." He literally drummed a
tune into a singer's consciousness; he transposed songs on the spot to suit
circumstances; and through it all he was learning. Going forth in the evenings to restaurants with a troupe of pluggers, Gershwin watched the audience. The sentimental "Gay-Nineties" period was over, the people responded
to action, spirit, "pep." And Gershwin began making experiments in trans-
lating this "pep" into his playing at Remick's. At the same time, he tried out
tunes of his own on the customers.

And then he heard some of Jerome Kern's tuneful music from *The Girl
From Utah!* This, on top of his intoxication over Irving Berlin's *Alexander's
Ragtime Band,* spelled the end of song-plugging days. He began to see the
possibilities in musical comedy music. He began to see the path that he would
follow.

And at eighteen, he saw music of his in print for the first time. It was the
song, *When You Want 'Em, You Can't Get 'Em, When You've Got 'Em,
You Don't Want 'Em.* Published by a rival firm, that of Von Tilzer, it was
in no way remarkable, but it showed evidences of an alertness and sensitivity
to word-music that the genuine song writers from Mozart, Schubert, Mussorgsky down through Gershwin have shared. The music caught the spirit of
the words, the inflection, the humor.

In *The Passing Show of 1916,* Gershwin was represented with one song,
Making of a Girl. Imagine his feelings when he saw his name on the cover
of a show-piece for the first time. This *was* on the way! Then came a piano
piece in collaboration with Will Donaldson called *Rialto Ripples,* this one
published by Remick in 1917.

At the end of two years, Gershwin had grown out of Remick's, though he
always spoke with gratitude of the experience. Going to his manager, one
day, he announced that he was leaving, whereupon, that gentleman asked
him where he was going. And Gershwin replied, "I do not know. But something is taking me away."

Then for a day, Gershwin played the piano at Fox's City Theatre on Fourteenth Street in New York City. Just for a day, for at the first performance, after sailing smoothly along for several numbers, he lost his way in reading the manuscript-copy of one of the songs. The comedian in the act for which he was playing, realizing the situation, decided to have some fun at the new piano player's expense. "What makes you think you can play the piano?" The chorus girls giggled, the audience burst into gales of laughter, and George Gershwin, sick at heart, walked out of the theater for good, once the performance was over. Scarcely ten years later, he enjoyed sweet revenge when he signed a hundred thousand dollar contract with Mr. Fox, but *nothing* ever erased the comedian's face from his memory.

Meanwhile, still groping his way, after almost becoming Irving Berlin's secretary—a mistake avoided by their combined good sense—Gershwin attracted the attention of Max Dreyfus, of the Harms Publishing Company. Dreyfus, who had a "talent" for picking talent, announced to Gershwin: "I think you have it in you and I'm willing to gamble on it—to the extent of thirty-five dollars a week until it comes out. All you need do is appear every morning, then go about your business. We'll see what we shall see."

And Dreyfus knew what he was doing. The song *I Was So Young, You Were So Beautiful* started the ball rolling. Then, from this new partnership, came *Half Past Eight,* an ill-fated show that never reached New York, and did little more than grant our young hero the satisfaction of seeing "Music by George Gershwin" on the billboard. Following that, Alexander Aarons, at the recommendation of Dreyfus, commissioned Gershwin to write a musical comedy. It was too good to be true, but there was the contract! And thus George Gershwin's first musical comedy, *La La Lucille,* gay-hearted and tuneful, came into being and had its official opening on June 12, 1919, at the Colonial Theater in Boston. It received a warm welcome there, and was equally popular during the hot summer months in New York.

Meanwhile, Gershwin's song *Swanee,* which had been sung at the Capitol Theater in New York without undue notice, attracted the attention of the comedian, Al Jolson. He adopted it "as his own," and, thereby, *Swanee* and George Gershwin became famous overnight.

Like magic, Gershwin music came into demand: A song for this show, another for that. *Waiting for the Sun to Come Out* went into *The Sweetheart Shop; Snow Flakes* and *Spanish Love* appeared in *Broadway Brevities; Some Rain Must Fall, Dancing Shoes* and several others in *A Dangerous Maid*—to mention just a few.

Then in 1920 Gershwin—on his way—did not walk but leapt into fresher fields, when he was chosen by George White to write the music for his *Scandals*. This exciting commission continued for five successive years, the pinnacle of the journey occurring in *The Scandals of 1922*. In that show were: *I Found a Four Leaf Clover, She Hangs Out In Our Alley, Across the Sea, Where Is the Man of My Dreams* and then, for those who saw that production, the glamorous spectacle of *I'll Build a Stairway to Paradise*, played by Paul Whiteman's orchestra, rocking the theater into a frenzy with George Gershwin's jazz spirit in music.

The opening night performance of this *Scandals* also contained Gershwin's one-act jazz opera, *Blue Monday Blues*, written to words by Buddy de Sylva. Though regarded by a few as a unique experiment, most of the critics did not care for it, and agreeing that, perhaps it did not belong in an evening of light entertainment, George White withdrew it after the opening night.

Gershwin was then commissioned to write the score to *The Rainbow Revue* for an English producer, but stifled by the thought of an unfamiliar audience, he did not write *Gershwin* music; and consequently, it turned out to be undistinguished music.

But jazz music was fast becoming a legitimate part of American culture. In fact, on November 1, 1923, jazz stepped into the portals of the select-ones, when Eva Gautier, a distinguished singer, gave a unique recital at Aeolian Hall. On her program was an All-American group of songs including *Alexander's Ragtime Band, Swanee* and *I'll Build A Stairway to Paradise*. Gershwin also made his debut as a concert pianist that night. It was, indeed, a memorable evening from which George Gershwin emerged, the King-Composer and Player in the now *respectable* jazz idiom!

And the year closed with his musical comedy *Sweet Little Devil*. He was now sitting on top of the world. Jazz had become the vogue of the intelligentsia. Gershwin had become the high priest of jazz and then, Paul Whiteman gave jazz and Gershwin the one extra boost that resulted in the *Rhapsody in Blue*. Whiteman, determined to raise jazz from its Tin Pan Alley associations into the realm of concert music, planned a concert of jazz music to be given at Aeolian Hall. He asked Gershwin to write something for the program. Busy at the time, Gershwin decided that he could not accept the offer. Imagine his surprise, when he read, in a newspaper at the beginning of 1924, that George Gershwin was at work on a symphony. He'd better get busy at it!

And pondering over the misconceptions of jazz rhythms, of what jazz was and what it was not, he hit on the idea of setting down these thoughts in music, higgledy-piggledly, without form or reason. Carrying these themes in his head during a trip to Boston, he became conscious of the steel-grinding, rattledy-bang rhythms of the train as it moved along. He began to hear the rhapsody as a whole—a musical kaleidoscope of America—with its mixture of peoples, its vitality, its blues, its city-madness—*Rhapsody in Blue*.

Paul Whiteman was overcome with emotion when he began to rehearse the work. And on that famous night of February 12, 1924, once he had recovered from fright at this daring venture that he had launched in Aeolian Hall, Whiteman enjoyed the spectacle of high-brow critics and serious music lovers responding to concert-jazz. And as everyone knows, *Rhapsody in Blue* made musical history that night.

Next, Gershwin wrote the successful show, *Primrose*, for England. Then came *Lady Be Good*, the first musical comedy in which George and Ira Gershwin completely collaborated. And this genuine collaboration made of *Lady Be Good* a rare thing. Words and music, with their inflection as one, captivated the audiences then, and kept the world dancing thereafter—to *Fascinating Rhythm*, *Lady Be Good* and *So Am I!*

The Song of The Flame came next, then *Tip Toes*, though it had been written previously. *Oh Kay* followed, a show that literally lifted colloquial speech into music; then *Strike Up The Band*, *Funny Face*, *Treasure Girl*, *Show Girl*, *Girl Crazy*, all topped off with the Pulitzer-prize winning *Of Thee I Sing*. Just to mention the names, evokes a spirit of Gershwin's music!

199

On December 3, 1925, Gershwin's Concerto in F, commissioned by Walter Damrosch, was played at Carnegie Hall. In this, as in everything that is true Gershwin, its value lies in its freshness rather than its form.

As a famous young composer, Gershwin went to Paris in the spring of 1928. There he was fêted in royal fashion: many concerts of his music were given, and wherever he went, there went the *Rhapsody in Blue*.

But before these festivities started, Gershwin enjoyed a week or ten days of relaxation, from overwork, with his friends—Mr. and Mrs. Robert Schirmer. They were occupying the apartment of Waldo Pierce, the noted American artist, and the location completely satisfied George Gershwin's dream of *Paris*. Situated on the Left Bank, directly opposite the Place Vendôme, it required but a short walk across the bridge and through the Tuileries Gardens to reach the Rue de la Paix where the banks, patronized by American tourists, were located.

During the first few days of his visit there were many opportunities to chat about his work—about what he had been doing, and what he planned to do. He wanted to write an opera, and he was tempted by the "Dybbuk" subject; he also spoke of writing a string quartet; and he discussed the possibility of studying harmony and composition with some outstanding modern composer—Ravel—or possibly, Alban Berg, whose music he greatly admired.

"If only I could get time—I mean a year or so—to do the study I want to, I could write all these things," he told his friends.

And then one bright, sunny morning, he went out by himself to cash a check, or pick up his mail; for though unfamiliar with the city, he could manage this little cross-the-bridge jaunt. Returning in a bit less than an hour, before joining his host and hostess at lunch, he sat down at the piano and began to thump out an intriguing tune with one finger. "What do you think that sounds like?" he asked his friends.

"I have no idea, but it's amusing," answered Robert Schirmer.

And George Gershwin said, "Well, to me it just sort of represents the way I felt when I was walking through the Tuileries Gardens just now."

During the next few days he played the theme—with more than one finger

200

—several times. And then one day, he said, "You know that would make a theme for some kind of symphonic sketch. Why not call it 'An American in Paris'?"

That is how the "First Walking Theme" of the tone poem, *An American in Paris,* came into being!

Soon afterward, he went to Vienna for the express purpose of seeing Alban Berg, but since Berg spoke only German, and Gershwin, only English, the meeting had slight consequences. From Vienna he went to London, where he was joined by Ira and his wife, and the Gershwins' sister Frances. Journeying to Paris in time for the Paris premiere of the *Rhapsody in Blue,* they took large and comfortable quarters at the Hotel Majestic where Gershwin began to work steadily on his *An American in Paris.* One day, during this time, remains fixed in Mr. Schirmer's memory—the taxi-horn-day. Gershwin insisted upon having just the right taxi-horn sounds for his score. Off they went down the Avenue Wagram—filled with automobile accessory salesrooms—to find the proper horns. One after another, they tooted and squawked, to find the right pitch, until the salespeople, shaking their heads, muttered, "those crazy Americans."

And thus *An American in Paris* grew, until, by the time Gershwin left Paris, four-fifths of the piano-score had been finished.

Later, Gershwin went to Hollywood, where he wrote his *Second Rhapsody;* and year by year his reputation grew. But one idea continually tormented him: he must write an opera! Truth to tell, he had hopes of writing *The American Opera.* After various experiments, he decided on DuBose Heyward's novel *Porgy* for his libretto.

With rare humility, sensitivity and artistry he set about his task. It should not be copied after Wagner's operas, Verdi's operas, or anyone's operas. And since he wanted the full tissue of the music to be genuinely individual, he worked conscientiously at the study of orchestration—that of Berlioz, Rimsky-Korsakov and others—in order to have the tools at the command of his ideas. And in order to know his characters, he lived in their community for a year.

Porgy and Bess was given its first performance by the Theatre Guild in

201

New York City on October 10, 1935. The air along Fifty-Second Street was electrified that night. And a treat was in store for those fortunate enough to get into the theater. From the beginning note of the score, the music was exciting, as it swept magically along—*Summertime, A Woman Is a Sometime Thing, I Got Plenty of Nuttin, Bess, You Is My Woman Now, It Ain't Necessarily So*—until, with Porgy, in *Where Is My Bess*, singing with Gershwin that he was on his way, the curtain went down on a "task" well done.

The critics disagreed on the merits of this opera, some of them even asserting, that, in form, it was no opera. But form or no form, it possesses what many an accepted opera does *not* have—life!

Following *Porgy and Bess*, Gershwin was commissioned to write music for the films, and in that capacity went out to Hollywood, where, he wrote the music for: *Shall We Dance, Damsel in Distress* and the Goldwyn Follies.

Then after an unsuccessful operation, he died in Hollywood, on July 11, 1937.

It did not seem possible. Gershwin, so full of life, and giving so much of life, could not have stopped living. And he had not. For his music, ringing in the Lewisohn Stadium, appearing suddenly over the radio, or just creeping into the memory, carries the spirit of America on its way—always groping, but growing—towards freedom, towards life—*Dawn of a New Day!*

INDEX

203

204

206